JACKIE HALL

What's in it
FOR ME?

Disclaimer: The intent of this author is only to offer information of a general nature to help you in your quest for emotional well-being. It is not intended to be a substitute for any psychological, financial, legal, or any other professional advice. In the event you use any of the information in this book for yourself, the author and publisher assume no responsibility for your actions. If expert assistance or counselling is needed, the services of a competent medical or psychological professional should be sought.

First published 2013

2013 © Jackie Hall

All rights reserved. Without limiting the rights under copyright restricted above, no part of this publication may be reproduced, stored in or introduced into a retrieval system, or transmitted, in any form or by any means (electronic, mechanical, photocopying, recording or otherwise), without the prior written permission of both the copyright owner and the above publisher of this book.

Edited by Louise Johnson

Cover Design by Allan P. Ytac

ISBN-13: 978-0-9875433-3-2

Disclaimer

The intent of this author is only to offer information of a general nature to help you in your quest for emotional well-being. It is not intended to be a substitute for any psychological, financial, legal, or any other professional advice. In the event you use any of the information in this book for yourself, the author and publisher assume no responsibility for your actions. If expert assistance or counselling is needed, the services of a competent medical or psychological professional should be sought.

TABLE OF CONTENTS

INTRODUCTION 1

Section A - Understanding the Problem

1. THE ROOT CAUSE OF CONFLICT 13
2. THE CORE BELIEF BEHIND ALL STRESS, EMOTION, DEPRESSION & ANXIETY 22
3. GENDER CONFLICT - UNDERSTANDING THE DIFFERENCE BETWEEN MEN AND WOMEN IS VITAL FOR HEALTHY RELATIONSHIPS 27
4. UNDERSTANDING YOUR PARTNER'S VIEWS ON LIFE 58
   Exercise One - Understanding Yourself and Your Partner 61

Section B - The Reality of Your Current Relationship

5. TAKING THE FIRST STEPS TO CHANGE: PERSONAL RESPONSIBILITY 83

   Exercise Two - Self-Reflection:
   How is Your View of Life Affecting Your Relationship? 89

   Exercise Three - Self-Reflection:
   how have you taught your partner to treat you? 99

6. LETTING GO OF THE BLAME GAME 101
7. PLAYING YOUR PART IN THE SOLUTION 122
8. FOR WOMEN:
   WHAT MEN WANT & HOW TO GIVE THEM MORE RESPECT 128

9. FOR MEN:
   WHAT WOMEN WANT & HOW TO GIVE THEM MORE LOVE............159

10. WHEN TWO WORLDS ALIGN..170

Section C - Creating Change in Your Relationship

11. INTIMACY –
    THE REAL AGENDA BEHIND ANY RELATIONSHIP...................185

12. PREPARING FOR CHANGE.
    SETTING THE FOUNDATIONS FOR ALIGNING YOUR RELATIONSHIP........191
    Exercise Four - What is the Real Problem?......................197
    Exercise Five - What Do I Want?..205

13. EFFECTIVE COMMUNICATION STRATEGIES...........................209
    Communication Tips for Men Talking to Women.............218
    Communication Tips for Women Talking to Men.............223
    Exercise Six - Communicating Differently.......................227

14. UNDERSTANDING, NEGOTIATION & COMPROMISE...............229

15. CREATING A NEW AGREEMENT –
    A ROAD MAP FOR SUCCESSFUL COMMUNICATION,
    NEGOTIATION & COMPROMISE..241

16. THE MIND TRACK TO HAPPINESS PROCESS...........................250

17. CONCLUSION 257

INTRODUCTION

As I write this book my husband Steve and I have been together for 17 years. He was 21 and I was 18 when we met, so for almost half of my life I have lived with this gorgeous, loving man - we moved in together just six months after getting together.

For the most part our relationship has been very strong and open, but had it been left up to me to guide it in this direction I know without a doubt it would've ended in failure long ago.

I credit so much of what I can teach you in this book to what my husband Steve has been able to teach me over the years and for the love and connection we have managed to maintain through some difficult times.

I am the first to admit he has moulded me from a feisty, argumentative, domineering partner who always needed to have the last word, into a more rational, even tempered, open minded partner who no longer runs out slamming doors in an irrational temper and who now only occasionally needs to be right.

This book is definitely not written from a pedestal of perfection. I am a work in progress - as we all are.

I am testimony that first impressions don't last. When Steve first laid eyes on me it was far from love at first sight. I was in amidst of one of my "I'm so tough" tantrums. A friend of the family had accidentally knocked a drink out of my hands onto the ground and I was giving him a serve, publically and loudly.

Steve vividly recalls saying to my friend, "Oh my God, who is that stupid bitch." Ouch!

Thankfully that wasn't the end of our dealings and as I got to know him and he got to know me better, he obviously saw something else in me because we eventually ended up together and never parted ways.

I remember when Steve and I had one of our first arguments. I got angry and in my usual fiery way, went to leave. My usual exit would have been ridiculously dramatic, throwing my car into reverse and screeching my tyres down the street so everyone would know I was angry.

However, this particular day Steve laughed. Not in a patronising way, but in an amused way. He lovingly said to me: "Where are you going? Come back here and talk to me."

I remember being confused by his reaction. Hang on, I'd never got this sort of response before. I was looking for the fight and the drama. It was what I thought was the way to have a relationship - either being the submissive one who was being dominated or the aggressive one who had to stand her ground. But this?

I hadn't considered the possibility of rationally talking things out. No one had ever taught me to do that before. That was just a strange concept to me.

So I stayed and it worked. We talked. He listened. I listened to him and we worked out the issue.

This was just the start of me learning a completely new way to have a relationship, very different from what I'd known from my childhood.

Over the years of being with Steve I learnt how to communicate, negotiate, compromise and love another person without all that drama and conflict.

Even though externally we have had our hardships to deal with, like anyone has, I have always felt great pride in being able to say Steve and I have pretty much always had a close and open relationship that seems to be getting stronger. While initially it was Steve's direction that brought us closer, it is now a combination of what I've learnt through personal development and my career, and his innate ability to love.

As a life coach I help people understand and deal with their own emotions and learn how to interact with their relationships, so it wasn't a strange mission for me to write a book like this.

When I first began writing on this topic it was my intention to help readers to gain a deeper approach to understanding their behaviour and their partner's behaviour by learning how to understand the thinking behind that behaviour.

Many resources out there just focus on negotiation, communication and compromise in a relationship, but I wanted to take things one step further and give you a more psychological perspective on your relationship.

Through my learning, and applying it firsthand in my own relationships, I have found that the understanding of what is happening for your partner, and the games you both play with each other, can quickly help you ascertain the changes you need to make to create a more fulfilling relationship.

As a life coach for clients with stress, depression, anxiety, addictions and parenting issues, I have ventured into many conversations about relationships with both men and women and have a very solid understanding of the thinking behind many relationship issues and conflict.

It was my intention to take what I had learnt from my experience as a life coach, combined with what Steve has taught me over the years and the insight I've gained from observing the dysfunctional aspects of my mother's relationship with my father and step father, and turn it into a book with loads of beneficial information for you to implement into your life.

However, as I began to write this book I had no idea it would morph into such a massive topic. Through my research into the way men and women think I stumbled upon a massive epidemic in our society – our confusing and conflicting gender roles.

I already knew women were under a lot of pressure in today's society and from my experience working with male clients I was also aware there were a lot of troubled men out there too. However, the conflict within ourselves and our gender roles is having a hugely detrimental effect on our relationships.

After researching and then seeing these issues in every relationship I come across, I am convinced that both sexes have some serious work to do in repairing ourselves as well as our relationships.

I quickly realised the book I was going to write on relationships was going to be quite different to anything I had ever written before. For once I was venturing into something that could be seen as controversial.

Usually I stick to factual information that most people can adopt. And although this book follows the same evidence based approach I normally take, *What's in it for me?* is likely to be more open to interpretation and opinion in some places. By giving you several examples and contexts to receive this information, it is my hope for you to become open to the concepts presented.

I admit that while writing this book I came up against many brick walls. Does this apply to this sort of couple? Does this information work for the couple going through that problem? I was barely able to have a conversation with Steve or any other couple without analysing what was going on within the dynamics and whether it fit in with what I was writing about.

I really wanted to write something that related to everyone, yet was aware there were so many different opinions, beliefs and lifestyles to contend with.

I wanted to stay true to my reality based informative approach, yet could not neglect to include the social and gender conflicts I stumbled upon which I have come to believe is crucial to the understanding and correction of marital relationship issues.

As is usually the case with any non-fiction book, this book is the amalgamation of experiences, ideas and approaches formed by an author

INTRODUCTION

who hopes that by presenting the information she will open her reader's mind and offer information that will be of benefit to their life, and in this case their relationship.

Feel free to take on whatever information you find that works for you and glaze over the stuff that doesn't. However, I urge you to test some of the concepts that are new to you even if they don't seem like they are relevant or if you don't like the gender stereotypical nature of them. You may be surprised by the results you get, just as I have.

You have probably come to this book because you are either experiencing many difficulties or one big issue with your partner.

A word of warning - I won't just be showing you how to deal with your partner's behaviour. I will also be helping you to deal with your own. It's important you come into this book with an open and honest mindset, willing to look at your own part in the problems between you and your partner.

Chances are you are quite stuck in your ways and so is your partner. Chances are you may have a lot of resentment to work through that comes not only from your interactions and treatment of each other, but from resentment and issues that occurred long before you were even together.

Relationships always come with baggage and take work - the reality is that it's nothing like the fairy tales we all grew up to believe were true.

You have to be willing to step up and be the beacon of change, often when your partner is NOT changing, because someone has to make the effort. Someone has to be the hero of your relationship.

Too often we get caught up in viewing our partner as the enemy, but when we look at the situation closer with the right magnifying glass we may find there is a much more amicable way to solve our issues.

The reality is relationships are made up of two individuals with two different belief systems. Each individual's belief systems change and grow as their experiences impact and influence their lives.

In addition our gender roles are strong and are often deeply ingrained on a genetic level. The gender aspect also requires understanding and a sensitive approach. We often scoff at the differences between men and women, but still go on in our lives having no idea how to deal with the opposite sex.

After doing all the research for this book and combining it with my many years of counselling and coaching experience, this book now aims to give you a much deeper understanding of your partner and yourself and how deeply ingrained beliefs (yours and your partner's) are really the cause of your relationship issues.

From this much deeper understanding you will find the way in which you approach negotiation, communication and compromise completely changes.

With this in mind, this book has been set out into three very important sections:

PART A: UNDERSTANDING THE PROBLEM

This section helps you to understand the deeply ingrained beliefs behind yours and your partner's behaviour. It helps you to stop personalising their behaviour and deal with the real issue.

What's in it for me? teaches you to understand how the brain thinks and how both you and your partner are actually after the same things in life, you just go about life in a different way.

We also look at the very stark contrasts between how a male thinks and how a woman thinks and why this is causing so many problems in our relationships. You will see how both of you have had these thinking approaches heavily ingrained in you through the events of history.

INTRODUCTION

Part B: The reality of your relationship

Part B will bring your attention back to the reality of right now and helps you make sense of your relationship problems.

Why are you experiencing problems in your relationship? How have you contributed to the current dynamic of your relationship? How can you let go of past behaviour and actions your partner has made? How can you play a part in the solution?

In this section you will be looking at how to take your understanding of the problem and accept it as your current reality.

Behind all stress, depression or anxiety is a conflict with the reality of what you are currently experiencing in life. When it comes to relationships we can harbour a lot of resentment and judgement towards our partner, stopping us from being able to move forward to finding solutions.

Forgiveness, understanding the current dynamic of how you treat each other, letting go of blame and freeing your attention up from dwelling on past events and instead focussing on solutions is what this section is dedicated to teaching you.

Part C: Creating Changes in your relationship

Parts A and B have been the foundation to applying more traditional approaches to making crucial changes in your relationship. Communication, negotiation and compromise are all very well-known skills needed to help us create our ideal relationship. Except now you will have a very different understanding of your partner to work with.

You will learn to use these skills with a very thorough knowledge of the belief systems that drive you and your partner and your *'What's in it for me?'* agendas. You will be able to understand and relate to their feelings more, recognise your own insecurities, fears and worries in their beliefs and approach your problems in a much more compassionate way.

Part C helps you prepare for change, learn how to communicate effectively, negotiate for what you want, and help your partner to get what he or she wants. It will help you to know when to compromise and when to stand your ground and how to create a new agreement with your partner.

By the end of this section you will have learnt a five step process to help you to know exactly what to do whenever you are faced with any problem in your relationship, forever.

Continuous communication, negotiation, compromise and new alignments are vital and obvious things we need to address whenever relationship issues occur. What gives these topics more depth and meaning and will thus create a deeper connection between you and your partner, is the addition of understanding and acceptance.

Understanding of the core beliefs that drive your partner and why they are important to him/her.

And acceptance of the idiosyncrasies that make your partner who they are and a willingness to work *with* them.

To get the most out of this book it will require you to be loving, compassionate and flexible. It will require an ability to step out of the two viewpoints:

- 'it's all about me'; and
- 'poor me'

With a very high divorce rate in society there has never been a more important time than now to become more aware of how to create a close and loving relationship that works for both you and your partner.

As parents we are faced with a decision that not only affects ourselves and our own fulfilment, but one that effects what our children are learning from us right now.

Do we continue to stay in loveless, nasty or dysfunctional relationships, stuck in the way we've always done things because we don't know any other way, and therefore risk seeing our children recreate those same dysfunctional relationships?

Or do we deliberately learn how to do things differently? Do we break the cycle of our parent's dysfunctional relationships (which is where you've likely learnt it) and recreate the relationship you desire by educating yourself with a different way of relating to your partner?

There is never any right or wrong way of doing life, only ways that produce a result. So which result would you prefer?

This book will present you with a way to help you and your partner to align on how you would both like your relationship to be. One that will produce the results of a loving, fulfilling and friendly relationship that you want to continue to nurture and grow.

So are you ready to face the truth of how to build that connection, love and respect in your relationships?

Section A

Understanding the Problem

Chapter One

THE ROOT CAUSE OF CONFLICT

Relationships can be a big mystery to us, especially when we struggle to understand the other person.

Why do they behave like that? Why do people choose to do hurtful or antagonistic things to one another when they know it is hurtful or antagonistic? Why do people make the 'wrong' choice when they are fully aware of the 'right' thing to do?

In the marital arena men and women are asking themselves the same questions over and over again.

Women may question why men aren't more available for them or their family, why they won't listen, or help more, be more affectionate, more considerate or be a better role model?

Why can't they want less sex, be more attentive, be happier, stop working so much, help more around the house and be calmer and not so angry at life?

"Why?? That's my question. Why, why, why? Lol" says mum Anita when I asked on my Facebook page what my likers would like to know about relationships. *"Why do they find it hard to stick with what they say they will do?"*

Why when you have tried to talk to him a million times about doing something different and even gotten his agreement to change, does he still do the same frustrating things? He knows what he needs to do, yet he seems to forget or not care. Why won't he try harder and compromise more?

Men are completely baffled too.

Why do women nag all the time? Why is she never happy? Why is she always trying to change me? Why is she so uptight about the housework? What's the big deal about having a beer with the boys every now and again?

Why does she have to talk so much? Why doesn't she just say what she means? I never know what the right thing is to say. Why can't she just leave me alone? Why doesn't she understand that I'm trying to work and provide for the family? Why is it that what I do is never enough for her?

It is clear men and women are grossly misunderstanding each other and this is reflected in how many couples are heading for the divorce courts.

UNDERSTANDING HOW WE PERCEIVE LIFE

The way men and women think are completely different and we are going to spend quite a bit of time later in the book understanding those differences. Before we do I want to give you an overview of the way all humans think.

This will begin to help you realise what's going on behind your partner's behaviour and get insight into understanding them, particularly when they've closed up and won't talk to you.

It will help you to start understanding the motives of your partner and how your relationship has come to be the way it is.

When you are born your brain has very few neural connections. Neural connections are the pathways between one information cell and another (the connection between neurons).

As babies we generally have enough connections to help us with basic human functions – eat, sleep, heart rate and so on.

The rest of our neural connections are learnt from our environment, primarily from the age of zero to seven.

During this time we are learning from our observations, from self-experience and from being convinced by other people who we trust or who provide us enough evidence to adopt their ideas as beliefs.

The word evidence is highly significant when understanding why people think and act the way they do and it's a word you will hear a lot in this book. The brain is always looking for evidence to either reinforce your current beliefs, find good reason to doubt your beliefs or to change your beliefs.

How you perceive life is primarily learnt from your parents or primary caregivers. They are your first source of information. You watch them (observation), experience the cause and effect of their actions, either directly or indirectly (self-experience) and you adopt their beliefs because, as a child, you trusted them (convinced by others).

Observation, self-experience and being convinced by others are the three ways in which we learn.

Neural pathways and habits of thinking are formed through repetition. As you take on an idea and see evidence of that idea, thus becoming convinced by it, your brain establishes a connection between one idea and another. The more this happens the stronger the connection becomes.

The evaluation process

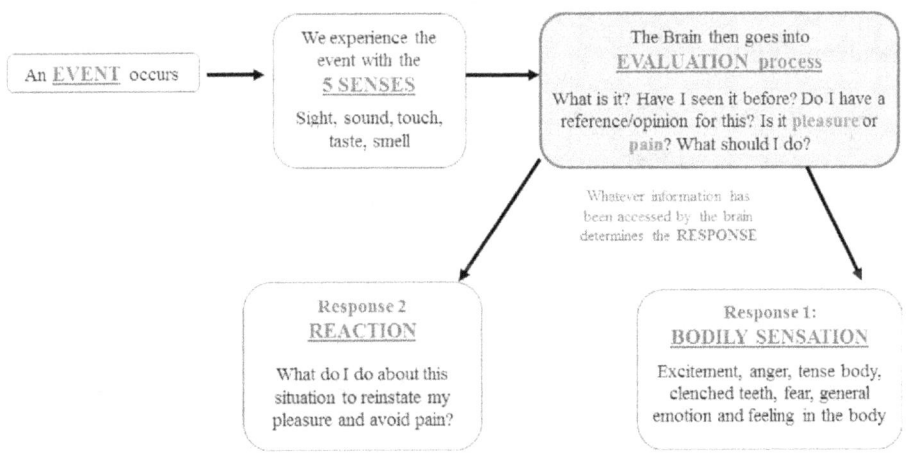

This is how the brain links and categorises information about life and you still use most of those early connections today. The reason you can walk, talk or use a spoon is because of the repetition of learning those habits and physically creating neural pathways in the brain.

To help clients to understand how the brain interprets life and how you and others think, feel and respond to life, I have created the evaluation process diagram found on the previous page.

We experience all events using one or more of the five senses. As the sensory information enters our brain we start a subconscious evaluation process.

The brain asks: What is this? Have I seen it before? Do I have a reference point (memory of a past event or an experience I can identify with) or an opinion about what I am experiencing?

The reason it is searching for meaning is to judge whether the event is pleasurable or painful and then to establish what to do about it.

In order to interpret what is happening the brain is using the already linked and categorised information that has come from all of the experiences you have had in life to date. Essentially the brain is calling upon information from your past.

How you interpret the event then determines the response you have to the event. Either:

a) The bodily sensations that we know of as our emotions, such as anger or sadness, or physical bodily sensations, such as sweating, shaking, clenched teeth, 'butterflies in the stomach' etc.

b) The re-action: What I physically do about the situation with the primarily agenda of restoring pleasure and avoiding pain.

Pursuing pleasure and avoiding pain is the primary goal of all human beings and thus what is behind all the decisions we make and the actions we take. This is what I will refer to as the 'What's in it for me' concept.

This highlighted sentence is going to be vital to understanding your partner's behaviour and your own behaviour, so I encourage you to go back and read it again. I will elaborate on this concept shortly.

When we take a look at much of the information attempting to help us to solve our relationship issues, much focus is put on trying to change the response stage of the evaluation process – either trying to stop the emotion or change the behaviour.

For example, if we are dealing with anger management we often learn how to stop the emotion of anger by using actionable (re-action) techniques like taking a deep breath or taking a step backwards.

If dealing with your child's challenging behaviour we often learn disciplinary techniques to stop their behaviour, like time out or diversion techniques.

When we are dealing with relationship issues we may learn how to change our partner's behaviour, how to communicate effectively and negotiate change.

None of these approaches are wrong, but they may be missing a very important ingredient that will provide long term changes.

These techniques have missed focussing on the cause of the problem in the first place – the evaluation process. The emotions you and your partner feel and your reactions to each other and to life are just the response stage of the evaluation process. The emotion and behaviour is just the end result.

If you want to change your partner's response to you, you have to work with their evaluation process. You have to understand its roots. You have to understand how their beliefs bring them pleasure or help them avoid pain. You have to understand their perspective so you can figure out how to reason and negotiate and compromise.

The cause of conflict in your relationship lies in how both parties are evaluating life. The solution to conflict is learning how to understand that evaluation and create alignment between what you believe and what they believe, respecting both points of view.

Using our previous examples, in the case of anger, taking a deep breath is helpful for dealing with that particular moment, but it only serves as a temporary fix until the same situation arises again, triggering the same beliefs (evaluation) and causing the same response (anger).

When dealing with your child's behaviour (their response) and their emotions, whether you yell at them to stop doing what they're doing or put them in time out, the same applies. It will only be a temporary fix until the next time a similar event triggers the same beliefs causing the same response.

When it comes to relationship issues it makes sense that regardless of what you do or say to change your partner's behaviour, you will likely receive the same response from your partner unless you understand and address the evaluation process behind theirs and your behaviour.

At the *Parental Stress Centre* rather than be another resource that adds to the tools to handle behaviour and emotion, we deal first with the evaluation side of things, focussing on how to change your perception of life which *automatically* changes how you respond to it.

Our *BE the Change Webinar Series* focuses on how you can change how you perceive your life and your self-worth and stop your bodily response of stress, depression and anxiety.

Our *Stress Free Parenting Webinar Series* focusses on how you can change how your child perceives life and their self-worth so your child's response (behaviour and emotions) automatically changes. This series teaches you how to create healthy minded, happy, confident children without having to resort to yelling, smacking and being far from the parent you want to be.

All of the books, resources and articles you will find at the *Parental Stress Centre* will educate you on how to understand the evaluation process behind why we behave the way we do and helps you to change that thinking.

This book is no different.

If you wish to make long term changes to your relationship and create the close, fulfilling relationship that you desire, you must understand how your partner is thinking and the real reason they are behaving the way they are.

You must be able to identify your own thinking which dictates your own emotions and behaviours so you can be more aware of how you too are contributing to the dynamics in your relationship.

You can't change what you don't acknowledge, so when you begin to understand the evaluation process causing the conflict in the first place and correct that, then you will start to see some real changes occurring within your relationship.

LEARNING HOW TO GET LIFE RIGHT

Earlier I mentioned the primary goal of all human beings is to pursue pleasure and avoid pain. It is instinctual, primal and has been going on since the beginning of mankind, although how we do this has obviously changed from the caveman days.

Now it tends to be focussed on emotional survival just as much as physical survival.

Neural connections are mostly set up during the first seven years of your life, so during this time you are also learning about how to pursue emotional pleasure and avoid emotional pain.

You learn, primarily from your parents or primary caregivers, how to be in the world, what to value, how to feel about yourself and what you need to do to gain attention, affection, approval, acceptance, to fit in – essentially how to feel loved and be lovable.

You learn this through how your parents spoke to you and your siblings and from your parent's relationships (or lack thereof). You received repetitive information about yourself from them that created neural pathways in the brain forming habits of thinking.

Over the years of being a child and learning about the world you will have also adopted certain beliefs on the right way to live and the wrong way to live. The repetition of these messages became cemented as beliefs about how to "get life right".

Most of us have a good understanding of the idea that our childhood is influential to our beliefs about life, but what you may not realise is that most of us are still operating through those very same perceptions of life and self.

You may have learnt to adopt beliefs that focus on what you can tangibly achieve to make you worthy – success, careers, money, status, marriages, children, cars, possessions, friendships, relationships etc.

You will have learnt through your repetitive experiences that living this 'right' way makes you worthy of love or approval and now because these beliefs have become physical neural pathways in the brain, you now perceive this 'right' life as the only way to live.

Most of us have also learnt to place our worth on the roles we play. As a child you learnt how to fit in. You may have established your place in the family by being the responsible one, the achiever, the good girl or boy, the oldest, the attractive or good looking one, or the smart one, to name a few of the labels we create for ourselves.

Even the 'not so nice' labels can over time become labels you still believe you need to live up to. Ever said to yourself 'this is who I am'? Character traits such as the dumb one, the non-academic one, the one that will never amount to anything, the loser, the one who always stuffs up, the black sheep of the family, or the failure, may be etched in your habitual definition of yourself.

Perhaps you became known as one of these 'not so nice' labels and this was your way of receiving acceptance or attention. It became a personality trait you believe defines you in the world and it has become how you fit in with society.

Although it's hard to conceive that living up to one of the 'not so nice' labels is occurring because you feel it somehow makes you worthy, it is still often the case. It usually comes from a fear of having nothing else to offer if you took that label away. "It's the only way I know how to be."

These labels may be the only way you feel you can receive attention or the only way you know to define yourself in the world. You've never been any other person than that label - and you have the evidence from your past experiences to prove it.

Both you and your partner will have adopted specific beliefs about the 'right' way to live and what your identity needs to be in order to be loved, lovable, accepted, to fit in or to have a successful life.

Understanding the beliefs you and your partner have become attached to will be an integral part of understanding the set-up of the dynamic between the two of you.

Understanding is the first part to creating change. Once you identify the set-up of the dynamic and what is driving that set up, you can then begin to repair your relationship through much deeper communication. Now you're not just working with the end result – the response. You are working with their deeply ingrained thinking set up long before you were even together.

Chapter Two

THE CORE BELIEF BEHIND ALL STRESS, EMOTION, DEPRESSION AND ANXIETY

As a society we live in a "get your life right" world.

As a child you first experience your parents who grew up with indoctrinations about the 'right way to live' from their own childhood experiences, some of which may be out of date with current society. You learn how to be worthy through what you see (observation) what you experience (self-experience) and being literally told (convinced by others).

Then the rest of the world reinforces what your parents taught you about how to be worthy.

We have an education system that bombards us with the pressure to succeed academically, which can easily teach us that *what you know* is an indication of your worth.

Religion often teaches how to 'get life right' and the consequences of judgement from the religion's deity if you get it wrong, teaching us that only the *'right behaviour'* will make you worthy.

Media headlines exploit those who got life wrong and continuously highlight 'bad' behaviour, casting judgement on that person or people and ostracising them.

Advertising campaigns paint pictures of the "right life" and tell you how your life will be more worthy once you buy their products and "get life right".

As a child we learn what we believe we should be, do or have in order to be loved, lovable or worthy. From here we continue to strive to meet the expectations, character traits and achievements we've learnt defines our worth and makes us important in life.

Look at all the evidence we have from our surrounds as a child and you will see there is no room for error. We learn to adopt an incorrect perception of self-worth because we live in a society that promotes worth as being conditional – get it right and I have succeeded. Get it wrong and I have ruined my life and possibly other people's lives too.

Getting life wrong makes us feel unloved, unworthy, unacceptable and unlovable. It causes us pain.

Our instinct is to avoid pain, so very early on you learn how to avoid pain by living up to those identities, successes and the "right life" you've been indoctrinated to believe is the way to live.

If I cannot reach my goals, live life the 'right' way or be received by others as living up to a certain identity or reputation then…

"I am worth-less"

The fear you could get life wrong and become worth-less or believing you already have gotten life wrong and are worth-less is the underlying belief that causes ALL stress.

This core belief is the culprit for creating the bodily response of all stress, painful emotion, depression and anxiety and is the same belief creating the behaviour (re-action) of criminals, violence and deliberate acts of harm to another person (emotional or otherwise).

Underneath a hateful person or a nasty act is just a human being hurting because at some level they believe they are worth-less or fear they might become worth-less, all because they've learnt through their experiences that worth is conditional.

The point I want you to get to before you even begin to negotiate or communicate with your partner about your relationship issues, is the reason you both behave the way you do is because of these deeply ingrained self-worth beliefs.

You are both the same. Both of you are just trying to make your way in the world and feel loved, lovable, accepted and acknowledged. I want to teach you to be able to look behind your partner's behaviour and get a deeper understanding of how they're viewing life (their evaluation process) so you can begin aligning with them from that deeper understanding.

I have worked with drug addicts, alcoholics, violent men, people with high anxiety, criminals and severely depressed and anxious clients in my time, both men and women. In every single case fear of becoming worth-less or the belief they already were worth-less was always behind their behaviour. The same fear that deep down you and I have too.

Every client believed there were roles and expectations that had to be lived out in order to pursue the pleasure of love, acceptance and approval, or to avoid further emotional pain in the form of judgement, ridicule or potential failure.

And they didn't all have dysfunctional or traumatic childhoods to feel this way about life either.

One client grew up in what appeared to be a perfect childhood environment. His upbringing was on a farm, his parents had a wonderful and close relationship and he saw very little conflict within it. However he grew up to believe this is how he needed to live life in order for it to be successful, so when he came across difficulties or conflict he would rate his life as worth-less and go into depression.

Another client grew up in a very encouraging and academic family environment who never put any pressure on him to achieve, but he still adopted the belief that academic achievement defines worth and put a lot of pressure on himself to get good grades and pursue an academic career, even though it wasn't what he really wanted.

The belief *I am (or could be) worth-less* is the fundamental cause of all stress, painful emotions, depression and anxiety.

Let's try and understand the different levels of stress in our lives.

Minor Stress is when you believe an event is going wrong and is detracting from your life's worth, but once it is over so is the stress.

Psychological Stress is when you believe your whole life has not gone to plan and is now worth-less or heading in that direction and you don't know how to get back on track (and make it worthy again).

Depression is where you feel you have failed at life (or an area of it) and literally believe your life is worthless, not just worth "less", but worthless – I have nothing to offer.

Anxiety is where you are desperate to control life and prevent anything from jeopardising your "right life". You set loads of goals and micromanage everything, all with the underlying fear that if you don't get life right you will be worth-less.

Anger is about feeling like you've lost control of getting life right, or have lost your ability to play out the identity you are supposed to. It is an attempt to regain control or assert your power or the identity you have attached to your worth.

Understanding the beliefs behind behaviour helps you to see your partner's behaviour is not actually about you. It's about what they believe about themselves. You may just happen to trigger a response caused by those beliefs.

Often we try to discount our partner's opinions or views on a problem, but we don't realise the depth of why they hold onto those beliefs. They've had many years of believing what they believe, building solid neural pathways around them, and they don't just get changed easily.

In many cases your partner believes their very worth as a human being rests on them getting their own way.

If your partner is stuck in their ways about how to raise the children, how to keep the house clean, what to spend money on, and all of the other numerous issues couples fight over, there is a story that lies behind their stubbornness. There's a story about what they believe their opinion means about their life and their self-worth.

If your partner is a workaholic it will have something to do with beliefs about why there is a need to work so much.

If your partner is angry it will be about him or her feeling powerless about something in their life and they don't know how else to regain that power.

If your partner is suffering from depression or anxiety, they have beliefs about how life is supposed to go to get it right and they'll either be setting lots of goals in an attempt to control their life (anxiety) or they're exhausted trying to get life right and have lost motivation (depression). Perhaps they continue to swing between anxiety and depression and back again.

Chapter Three

GENDER CONFLICT
UNDERSTANDING THE DIFFERENCE BETWEEN MEN AND WOMEN IS VITAL FOR HEALTHY RELATIONSHIPS

Adding to the indoctrinated beliefs from our parents are beliefs from society about gender roles and expectations.

Possibly one of the biggest problems we have in marital relationships is that we don't really understand how the opposite sex views life and handles problems.

It's been about 21 years since John Gray's *Men are from Mars, Women are from Venus* hit our bookshops. Most of us know of the book and even snicker in recognition over the massive differences between our sexes, yet most of us never actually bothered to read it - at least not since having children and in context of our current relationship, let alone trying to apply it to our current problems.

I know I didn't read it until I began to do research for this book. I've had it sitting on my own book shelf for 10 years in my "one-day" pile. All I can say is WOW! I'm so glad I did. What it taught me about my husband's ways has been nothing short of transformational.

After reading that book, I then stumbled upon another transformational book called *Love & Respect* by Dr Emerson Eggerichs. This took my understanding even further. If you ever want to continue your understanding of relationships I would highly recommend reading both of these books.

What I realised after all my research, reading books, blogs and forums written by men and women, and from my experience working with clients, is just how often we fall into the trap of denying our partner what they need in the hope of getting more of what we need.

Eggerich's powerful book reveals a hidden secret (at least, it was a secret to me) that is the key to unlocking the balance and harmony that all relationships crave.

Women want love and men want respect.

I can't believe I'd not seen this before. It's so simple.

Often we think that more love is the answer to healing relationship hurts, but the love language of a male and a female are completely different.

Men, at some level, already know that a woman loves him. However, what he may not know is whether she likes him or values him. This is the respect and acknowledgement he's needing in order to become more loving towards his partner.

Women are focussed on receiving love, and finding evidence she is loved by her man helps her to be more respectful to her partner.

But over the years of neglecting this truth a nasty cycle can emerge.

She gets into the habit of saying: *"Why should I show him respect, when he doesn't show me any love or affection, doesn't care about me, does nothing for me, doesn't understand me, couldn't care less about me …"*

He gets into the habit of saying: *"Why should I do anything for her? She doesn't show me any respect. All she does is criticise me, put me down, doesn't acknowledge anything I do for her and generally makes me feel like crap …"*

Both partners stay in their mindset hoping that by denying their partner more of what they want, their partner might wake up, see the error of their ways and give them more of what they need.

However this approach only serves to strengthen the cycle, promote more unhappiness in both parties and grow resentment between the couple.

As Eggerich puts it: *"When a husband feels disrespected, it is especially hard to love his wife. When a wife feels unloved, it is especially hard to respect her husband."*

Part A of this book is all about grasping a complete understanding of your partner's evaluation process both on an individual level and from a gender perspective.

WHY MALES WANT RESPECT

Take a look at the history of the male gender roles and you will see they have been traditionally set up for the man to be the leader of the family, the protector and provider – the one to be looked up to and respected.

This is true from caveman days when men were the hunters and women gatherers, to native traditions where men were the teachers, the story tellers, tribal chiefs and decision makers. Before the industrial revolution men were out in the fields working, often with young sons beside them, teaching them how to be men and look after their women for when these sons would become the 'man of the house'. After the industrial revolution men were still the breadwinners and the sole providers of their family while the women stayed home to nurture their offspring. This was all happening not so long ago.

For generations dads have been the leaders, the decision makers, the primary 'go-to' person and the one who knew more about life. Remember being told to *'go ask your father'*? Even now I fall into the trap of asking my husband some random question and being surprised when he doesn't know the answer, or I will say to my kids, *"Ask dad. He'll probably know that"*.

Furthermore, men are the physically dominant species. Although women can build themselves up to be just as strong as men, traditionally they aren't. So the tendency to be the dominant sex is even built into a man's physical structure.

No matter what you've been taught to believe about current gender roles, it is difficult to dispute that men have grown up to define their worth by their ability to work, achieve, provide and protect their families and prove they can be an emotional and physical pillar of strength for their partner.

They have learnt these roles are their responsibility as a man and if they are a good enough man this will be reflected in the respect shown by their partner and by society. This identity of man has been contributed to by men and women equally.

And I believe this is still very deeply ingrained in our men today.

Exactly what specific achievements and accomplishments a man feels he needs to succeed at may vary depending on his upbringing and social and cultural influences. In the next chapter you will complete an exercise to help you to get an understanding of what influences you (if you are a man reading this) or your partner (if you are a woman reading this) to feel good enough and how you or he rates himself as a man.

I'm not buying into stereo-types that all men are meeting these needs through traditional work or money pursuits, because there are rising numbers of men who are just as happy to be living non-traditional roles, such as stay at home dads for example.

However, they too are still likely to have desires to receive respect from providing and protecting their family. It just may be in different ways.

As a general rule a man's self-worth is attached to success and accomplishments. When a man feels as if he is achieving something or providing value to his partner, he feels he is good enough, valuable and needed.

Feeling needed and good enough is very important to a man.

For generations men have also been assigned to the role of being the one with all the answers – like a leader is expected to. From this deeply learnt trait he has learnt to become the fixer and problem solver.

When a man engages in a conversation with a woman who is presenting him with a problem, he instinctively goes into 'fix it' mode. This is how he subconsciously proves himself - by being able to provide her with the answers, protect her from further hurt and make her happy. That's what has been firmly ingrained in his neural connections - to serve and protect his partner. However, as we'll discuss shortly, this is not always what she wants.

For those readers who do not believe their partner is trying to make them happy, bear with me - it will become evident soon enough.

When a man is faced with a problem of his own, he is likely to withdraw from life so he can think it over and find a solution. As John Gray from *Men are from Mars, Women are from Venus* says, they go into their caves.

He will become immersed in an activity that allows him to think about the problem in more detail. He may tinker with something mechanical or go and do something where he can be by himself, or in this day and age, he may immerse himself further in work.

If there are multiple problems he will focus on the most important one and during this time he can become very distracted, unable to focus, unable to multi-task and unable to be present or be high functioning in other areas.

If the problem seems too big he will often engage in activities where he can forget about his problems, like reading the news or playing games. He may even engage in an activity where he is solving another problem unrelated to him, like watching the footy for example. Men can find it relaxing to get passionate about the errors of judgment footy players make and highlighting how those footy players could have done it better.

When men are able to either solve their own problem, escape from their problem or solve someone else's problem, they feel better about themselves and come out of the 'cave', ready to handle life again.

As a general rule men don't talk about their problems with other people unless that person is necessary to solving their problem. Communication is predominately used as either an exchange of information or as a means to get help because they haven't been able to find the answer themselves.

While I realise this trend is changing and men are learning how to be more open, it is likely that a communicative man has already gone through a deliberate process of learning how to communicate or they are receiving enough respect from their partners to feel safe to talk about their feelings without the fear of failure or criticism.

Why females want love

The male role has changed dramatically over the years, but so has the female role. The female role has predominately been to love and nurture. She is naturally empathic and supportive and is generally the primary carer of her children, even in today's society.

As a general rule:

Women base the value of relationships on how they feel and the quality of their relationships.

As we know, most women are talkers. When they are faced with a problem they want to talk it out. But they often won't just talk about one problem, they will talk about many of the problems they have with their world.

They look for someone they can trust and then will want to talk in great detail about their problems in order to feel better. What they are looking for is support. When someone is listening to her and her problems in a supportive and empathetic way she feels loved and cherished.

She is looking for someone who will care and nurture her like she would care and nurture for someone else.

When a woman has loving, nurturing relationships around her she feels good about herself. When she is isolated and has no one to talk to about her problems, she feels unloved.

Feeling loved, cared for and cherished is highly important to women and they can easily misunderstand a male's tendency to go into his cave as an indication he doesn't care about her.

When a woman is stressed she responds emotionally and wants to talk and talk and talk. The more she talks, the better she feels.

Often if the stress is too much, she may find relief in talking to someone else about their problems. She can become emotionally invested in others' problems too as it makes her feel better about her own problems. She feels nurtured and cherished by providing help to the other person.

Women naturally want to be there for other people in a supportive role because that's what she would want from others when she is feeling that way.

So when she senses something is wrong for a man, she wants to talk to him about it and offer her support, because that's what she would want him to do for her.

However, he often doesn't want to talk. He wants to retreat into his cave and solve the problem himself.

How these two worlds of male and female collide

As a rule of thumb if a man wants help to solve his problem he will ask. To receive unsolicited advice can be interpreted as saying, *"I don't trust you. I don't think you're good enough or competent enough to solve this problem yourself"*.

He may get offended and feels disrespected. His rejection of her support makes her think she's not loved.

When a woman has a problem she will begin her natural process of talking to her man about it. She is looking for support. She is looking for understanding and empathy. The more support, understanding and empathy she gets, the more she feels loved, cherished and therefore important and valuable.

However, when a man hears her speaking about her problems he wants to fix them. It is how he defines his worth. He wants to be needed and attempts to use his 'expertise' to fix her problem. Even if it's not his area of expertise he thinks that by finding a solution to her problem it will make her happier.

When he's hearing her talk about her problems he's in solution finding mode and is unlikely to even be thinking about how she's feeling. He's just not wired that way.

She perceives it as meaning he's not interested in what she's saying. He can be perceived as being blunt, uncaring, black and white, not understanding, cold, opinionated and rude because of his approach to her problems. She feels invalidated by the solution he offers and perceives his response as being an indication that he isn't listening or doesn't care about her.

When she responds in anger or criticises how he has responded to her problem, he feels rejected and hurt that he has not been able to fulfil her needs and solve her problem. He feels worse because not only has he not been able to fix her problem, but he has made her even more upset, which makes him feel inadequate as a partner too.

As women often like to talk about all their problems at once this can become frustrating and overbearing for a man. His problem solving goes into information overload and he can't solve her problems quick enough. Even when he feels he is presenting a pretty good case of how to get over a problem, she is bringing up even more problems or appears to him as being dismissive of his expertise (therefore feeling unneeded or appreciated).

"It never ends! She's always whinging. I can never make her happy!" you might hear him say.

What he doesn't realise, is that for her, the process of just talking about her problems will make her feel better. If he was to listen with the odd 'hmm' and 'yeah I understand' here and there, she would go through that process and be hugely grateful for his support. She would feel loved.

However without this understanding he's likely to be feeling incredibly overwhelmed and starting to get angry with her because he's starting to feel unhelpful and failing at not being able to make his partner happy.

He's not feeling successful, not feeling like he is accomplishing anything and not feeling like he is achieving the goal of being a good partner – all the things he pins his self-worth upon as a man.

Women need to feel like they are not alone and their feelings are being validated with compassion, understanding and support. This is how they feel loved.

Yet men need to feel like they are needed and are successful in their knowledge, actions, achievements and problem solving abilities. This is how they feel respected.

When a man is facing a problem, women seem to have the ability to pick up on it fairly easily. They tend to have a sixth sense about these things - probably because we have spent hours talking about problems with our girlfriends - and have learnt to see the signs that "something's up".

But remember men often don't want to talk about their problems - they want to fix it themselves. Men discuss their problems primarily when they believe the other person can help assist with solving them. Unsolicited advice can be perceived as their women saying he is untrusted, incompetent or unsuccessful in fulfilling his role of being the fixer and problem solver.

When women pick up that men are experiencing a problem they try to get them to talk about it and discuss their feelings, and then they give them advice. They ask questions to get a better understanding of the problem and this can come across as interrogating or nosey.

However, she believes she is helping her man feel loved and cared for like she would if someone was responding to her problem this way. What she doesn't realise is that the opposite is happening. Her man is likely to be feeling invalidated, undermined or feel like he is being treated as if he is stupid.

Men don't want to be told what to do. They don't want women to tell them where to park, which direction to take, which knife to use to cut the chicken and what to do with the children. If he wants your advice he will ask for it purely because he has realised for himself that he couldn't find the answer and believes you have the answer.

That doesn't mean that a woman can't ask a man to do anything or have a right to ask for him to change. It just means she will have to do it in a way that doesn't make him feel invalidated or disrespected. This is something we will discuss further in Part C of this book.

A man feels most empowered and motivated when he is feeling needed and is able to show his abilities, when he is achieving and when he feels successful at solving problems. His partner's acknowledgement of his achievements will go a long way.

> **When men and women neglect to understand these fundamental needs about each other they fall into the trap of expecting their partner to react to problems in the same way they would. We expect them to think the way that we think. The reality is they don't!**

In fact, it seems we are the complete opposite and when we don't understand these key differences, the demise of the relationship begins.

Women continue to feel invalidated, unimportant, unloved, unsupported and rejected. Men are feeling the same, only for completely different reasons.

> **When both parties in a relationship are feeling this way, the demise of respect for a man and the demise of love for a woman starts to take hold, creating a nasty cycle of "I hurt you because you hurt me."**

THE DEMISE OF RESPECT FOR MEN

The role of a male used to be very clear - it was predominately to lead, provide and protect his family. This earned him a place as a respectable man in society.

However women's liberation, inflation, technology and numerous other societal factors over recent years have made the world a lot more difficult for a man to feel worthy.

Women have entered the workforce, either to help meet growing financial pressures or because they now have a choice to pursue their careers.

They are perceived as being just as capable, and sometimes even better, at traditionally male dominated roles and are often earning more or playing equally important financial roles in the family unit.

Equally on the domestic front roles have changed and more demands are being placed on a man to be responsible for household chores.

In order to be the achiever and thus successful (worthy) as a man in this day and age he now has to work, achieve, protect, provide, look after the kids while she works, share the load after they both come home from work and provide more support on the weekends. He must do more around the house as well as tend to his traditional tasks around the home.

Even if a couple are still playing traditional roles where she stays home and he goes to work, there is still pressure for the man to be more engaging with the family and help out around the house or risk being labelled a chauvinist.

In a situation where the man stays home and the wife works, the pressure may come from being able to prove he can do it just as well as a woman can.

The 'rules' of how to be a respectable man have changed and often the lines are blurred - it's just not as clear cut as it used to be.

With the enormous progress made through women's liberation there is no doubt women have climbed their way up in social standing, often making more money than men. They are known for being more organised, efficient, smarter and more capable in a lot of cases too.

Women have been taught they can do everything a man can do and are often out to prove they can do it better too.

Women lift heavy weights, play the same sports, work the same careers, have the same pay (in almost all cases), expect the same treatment and often take the same risks.

As Beyonce says:

> *Boy I know you love it*
> *How we're smart enough to make these millions*
> *Strong enough to bear the children*
> *Then get back to business*

But in the process of reaching all of these heights and claiming to do it just as well as the men do it, what are all the men doing?

If men have been basing their self-worth on traditional roles, yet women are now taking on this responsibility too, how are men generally feeling about their place in the modern world?

Is it possible women are starting to teach men that they're not needed? Are we portraying the image that we are better than them and thus beginning to treat men as the lesser gender, just as women were treated not so long ago?

Women often portray the image that we can do it all on our own and sometimes we even tell them that we'd prefer to do it ourselves - we think we can do it better or faster on our own.

Ever said to your partner, *"Oh just leave it. You're not doing it right."* Or *"It's quicker if I do it. You don't know what you're doing."* Is this a regular message women are sending men without realising it?

In a lot of relationships women are criticising their men, nagging and complaining when he's working too long, not doing enough around the house and putting pressure on him to do more of this, and less of that. Women may be completely unaware of just how often they are doing this.

My husband and I have a great relationship, however after recognising how important it is to respect a man, I also realised how much more of an effort I could make by not nagging and complaining. I didn't realise he was sometimes taking my complaining personally.

Perhaps a lot of men don't really know what they're supposed to do anymore to be that respectable man. Perhaps he doesn't really know what achievements and accomplishments will make him feel successful.

Perhaps the demise of respect has been compromised by these societal changes and could be a huge contributor to the rising dysfunction in today's marriages. He's not feeling needed or respected and thus doesn't want to give love.

Following is a classic example of how the depiction of a male role is evident of the demise of respect for a male.

I happened to catch a cartoon episode my kids were watching called – *The Amazing World of Gumball.*

Here's the tone of the cartoon.

The show revolves around the Watersen family. Gumball is the son and he has two sisters. The show centres around the interactions between Mum, Dad, Gumball, his sisters and their friends. It is always about the trouble they get into and how they get out of it.

Gumball's mum works and provides for the family. Gumball's dad doesn't work at all. He is depicted as the dumb one of the family who always gets things wrong and is often getting in trouble because of his stupidity. Mum often has to excuse or ignore his stupid behaviour or save his mistakes from family ruin. The jokes on the show are often about the idiotic remarks Dad makes and his inability to provide for the family. Interestingly out of the team of eleven writers for this show eight of them are male.

In the particular episode I watched, Gumball (the son) had been asked out on a date and he really wanted this girl to like him. The family were discussing the impending date at the dinner table.

After his sister alerts Gumball to the fact he should be freaking out because if he messes it up his potential girlfriend will never speak to him again, Gumball gets worried that she won't like him.

His mum consoles: "Don't worry sweetie, just be yourself. That's all a girl wants." Then she leaves the room.

Gumball's dad is sitting at the table with his arms crossed, shaking his head. He then leans across and says: "Listen, son. Ignore everything your mother just said. Women only think they want us to be ourselves because they don't know how wretched we actually are. All you have to do is think of someone really cool and attractive, and be them."

His sister then chimes in that he should just shower her with expensive gifts to win her over. Of course, Gumball doesn't have any money (just like his dad).

However his dad says: "You don't need money to show her a good time. Do you think I have money? No. Do you see your mother leaving me?"

Gumball says: "Yes, every day to go to work."

He ignores that statement and says: "Do you want to hear the secret kept for centuries by Watersen men?"

He then proceeds to get him new clothes (from the rubbish dump because it's free).

Then he goes to the ATM and tells his son that the machine will give him money for free and proceeds to put a credit card in the machine clearly marked 'Nicole Watersen' and extracts cash out.

How's that for the portrayal of a message about men to a child.

It gets worse though. Then Gumball goes and gets advice from his sisters for his date. The first sister attempts to teach him how to sit down and have a 'civilised' conversation with her and sets him up to practice with her dolls. He fails miserably and she kicks him out of her room.

He then goes to the other sister and she slaps him across the face, telling him that he needs to be prepared for the unexpected.

She sets up four cardboard pop ups for him to block (hit) and defend so he can be prepared for the unexpected on his date. One pop up is a mugger.

She asks: "What do you do if you were faced with a mugger?"

He says: "Call the police."

She says: "No! Wrong! You knock his block off!"

The second pop up is an ex-boyfriend. The third was a disapproving dad and the fourth was a teddy bear who didn't believe in love. In all cases he was instructed to act assertively and powerfully.

This depicts the role of the protector and tough, strong male.

So off he goes to his date, dressed as someone else, prepared to block anything in his strong asserted, confident way, taking on a completely different persona than he would normally.

When he gets to his date, as it turns out, he didn't listen to her properly. When she asked: "Do you want to come over on Saturday…?" He was so smitten by her and that question, that he didn't hear the rest of the sentence. "…It is my pet spider's funeral."

Now I realise that this cartoon will go over most kids' heads and most of it is probably to entertain the overhearing adults, but I think this portrayal of men as incompetent buffoons contributes to the demise of respect in a man and confuses men even further as to what women want.

What message do you think this is sending to children about males and females?

If I read between the lines, here's what I get:

Men are stupid, non-working, idiots who don't know anything about money, who don't listen and think women won't accept you the way you are. You need to be someone you're not for her to like you because really men are 'wretched' (Miriam-Webster dictionary defines wretched as: *deeply afflicted, dejected or distressed in body or mind; being or appearing mean, miserable or contemptible*).

Women are the workers and the smarter ones who want a man to love her and give her expensive gifts even when he doesn't work. She wants him to be someone that he's not, even though she says she wants him to be himself. She also wants him to be a strong protector, prepared for the unexpected and wants him to be able to hold a civilised conversation with her….even though she thinks he's stupid.

Now tell me why the male gender role isn't in trouble and why they're also confused about how to love a woman.

Right now, I'm guessing there's a lot of ladies reading this that may be vehemently disagreeing with what I'm saying. I'm guessing you are the one feeling hard done by and feeling like you are the one being mistreated. Don't worry, I'm not saying that women are solely to blame for the dysfunction of a relationship. I'll be getting to your mistreatment shortly.

However for now, I urge you to choose a different perspective and look around you at the portrayal of the modern day man. Listen to the way your friends talk about their husbands. Is it often derogatory or deeming them as incompetent, either jokingly or seriously? What about the male roles played on TV. Are they depicted as either being the tough hero or the stupid Neanderthal like Gumball's dad? Homer Simpson is another example.

Where are the clear rules of how a man can feel like a man without contempt or fear of contempt in today's world?

The reality is there is a lot of confusion about the male identity in today's society because it's not as clear cut as it used to be. There are lots of rules and judgement imposed on the men of today and I believe this ambiguity could be sending a lot of men (and thus dads) into mental illnesses like depression and anxiety.

The Australia Bureau of statistics reported in 2012 that although the overall suicide rate has decreased by 17 percent in the last decade, "*Suicide remains the leading cause of death among Australians between 15 and 34 years of age*" and "*Males account for approximately three in four suicide deaths*". (Australian Bureau of Statistics Media Release, 24 July 2012 - Suicide Rates down over a decade[1])

With this statistical information at hand one has to ask some big questions. Are there a lot of men struggling with their place in the world? Are men

---

1 http://www.abs.gov.au/ausstats/abs@.nsf/Latestproducts/3309.0Media%20Release12010?opendocument&tabname=Summary&prodno=3309.0&issue=2010&num=&view=

clueless about what they should do to fulfil their roles as respectable men?

Are they feigning their happiness and covering up how they really feel? Are they trying to use career advancement, money, material possessions or even their sexuality to earn status and validation? Are they constantly feeling like something is missing? Are they losing their ability to identify with what it even means to be a man amidst the judgement, criticism, put downs and gender imbalance?

Are men at a loss as to what they need to do regain their leadership in the family, or at least be a part of the leadership?

Take a moment to think about the change in the definition of a man over recent years.

He started as a leader, sole provider, protector, head of the family, the one who makes his wife happy, the 'go-to' person with the knowledge and expertise about life and essentially the controller of decisions of his family. He was someone who was naturally respected.

Now at best he most likely plays an equal role in the family and needs to consult with his partner on most things or succumb to her being the decision maker in an attempt to make her happy (or at least try to). Only that doesn't seem to be making her happy either.

Meanwhile he's still dealing with the pressure of modern day financial and material gain in a competitive world, fearing that he may be judged by his income, feeling incompetent (at managing both work and domestic matters) and not knowing what to do to feel good about himself.

Is all this pressure and the shift in the male identity literally killing them?

Remember what I said earlier about what causes depression (suicide comes from severe depression).

Depression is where you feel you have failed at life and literally believe your life is worthless, not just worth....less, but worthless – I have nothing to offer.

When someone becomes increasingly depressed with their lives they can start to become angry, bitter and selfish. If it is a man behaving this way it could be because he doesn't feel needed anymore, or never feels good enough in the eyes of his partner, or society in general.

What do men do when they have a big problem they don't know how to solve? They retreat into another activity to forget their problem. He believes he may as well go and do something else to feel better about himself.

He may plan more boys' weekends away or hobby time where there's no one to judge him or criticise him. He may spend more time at work. Perhaps he does feel respected by his work colleagues.

My husband admitted to me that when the kids were young and I was in my throes of depression and anxiety he would deliberately stay a little longer at work to prevent having to come home to me and deal with the chaos. He tells me many of his friends did the same.

Some men turn to drugs, alcohol or gambling to help them to escape. These mood changers help them to momentarily feel better about themselves and help them forget problems and have more fun. It's only when the effects wear off they find themselves back to the reality of life.

Some men turn to dating sites even though they're married, go to strip clubs, have affairs or just go to night clubs where they can get attention from the opposite sex - something they're not getting at home or to fulfil a void of not feeling good enough in general.

Some men resort to treating their partners badly, either emotionally or physically, in a feeble attempt to reinstate power or demand some respect. Perhaps that's how his father did it.

As Steve Biddulph in his book, *Manhood*, states: *"If you can't get love, get even. If you can't get love, I'll make life worse* [for you] *in an attempt to feel better about my life."*

This is an extreme scenario and I'm by no means saying all men respond to life in this way. However with suicide rates so high in men in particular it is vital I try to explain the obvious dysfunction occurring in men so both sexes can see what may be going on behind that behaviour.

Although not all men are neglecting their family responsibilities, engaging in self destructive activities and treating their women badly, it is likely the 'good guys' are still a little confused and lost as to what the right balance is of how to be a good male role model for their children and give their partners what they need.

In the space of one day I heard two different dads say to me they felt they had essentially handed their life over to their wives once they had children – my husband was one of them.

Steve explained to me how he had felt when we first had our children. I became the decision maker, the dictator and he was always trying to make me happy. In fact he felt like it had become the constant focus of his decisions about when to come home from work, what to do, whether to do something for himself of not, should he be doing more and how was I going to react to the decisions he made.

He said he was continuously trying to pre-empt what I might need, how to help, what to do with the kids and whether he was doing enough. He was working hard for the family but also trying to do more around the house and keep me happy.

He even adopted the mantra: *Happy wife. Happy Life.*

But as a woman who had learnt that she should be super mum, having it all under control, be organised and do everything, the pressure was getting to me and I was in the midst of depression and anxiety myself. I would be resentful of his time away and take my own dis-ease with my life out on him a lot of the time.

To him he was never making me happy and felt helpless and frustrated, adding to his own stress and anxiety during that stage of our lives.

I never realised until now the effect my problems were having on his natural instinct to want to fix my problems and how this added to his stress. I was complaining and venting about my life to him to try and feel better about my problems. I didn't understand he was frustrated and stressed because he couldn't fix me and make me feel better. As a result he retreated into working more.

We were making the same classic mistakes many couples make – responding to each other in ways we would expect someone to respond to us.

The other Dad I spoke to was a client of mine with a similar story to my husband. He is working with me to improve himself, as many dads reading this book are too.

He literally said to me *"I defaulted my life to my wife when we had children"*.

I couldn't believe that he was validating the very thing my husband had said to me that same morning! I asked him what he meant by that.

He explained she had become the dictator of how life ran. She decided how the house was run, how he should do things, what they would do, when and what to feed the family, if they were going to go out or not. She became the problem solver, the rule maker, the expert of the family – all the things males use to traditionally pride themselves on.

In essence she became 'the boss' and I realised in the midst of our conversation it was almost as if he had become another child – the older child responsible for the siblings, but still ultimately being under the command of mum.

Just like a child, and just like my husband, he was constantly trying to pre-empt what she wanted and try to predict what was the right way of doing things to keep her happy. He was often unsuccessful.

Noticing he wasn't doing it her way, she would put him down and treat him as incompetent or offer unsolicited advice and inadvertently make him feel she thought he was incompetent.

He would resent her telling him what to do and react angrily to her. Remember, telling a man what to do makes him feel disrespected and not able to prove he can fix the problem himself.

I realised his anxiety was caused by his need for approval from her and the mild fear he could get it wrong and receive her disapproval (along with more judgements and arguments) making him feel more disrespected.

The demise of respect a man is conditioned to need by many generations of having received it, is coming from both societal changes in the role of a male and female as well as changes in how women are treating them. This could be either maliciously (as a result of the 'you hurt me, so I'll hurt you' cycle) or completely obliviously due to a lack of understanding of how men think and what individual beliefs have been set up in a man's childhood.

The way women are treating men is often making him unable to give her the love she is looking for. Later in the book I will show you how this cycle can be broken.

THE DEMISE OF LOVE FOR WOMEN

I think it is also important at this point to recognise women are not exempt from the repercussions of this new societal trend either. They too are stuck in a generational gap between the old and the new.

I can almost hear women screaming at me saying: *"What about us? Never mind poor him. What about poor me? Who's the one having to work and look after the kids? Who's the one trying to do it all with very little help? Why does he get to go into his cave and have time out? Why should I feel sorry for him when my workload is through the roof, often because of him?"*

Women are becoming more powerful than they were 50 years ago, but that too is paying a price.

They are stuck in the old school of being the homemakers, the nurturers, the sole carers of their children and catering for their man's needs, and the new power world of the working woman who can do anything a man does – and she has learnt she should be able to effortlessly handle it all.

Women are taking on a lot more of a work load, not just because they want to, but in many cases because they have been conditioned to believe they *have* to!

Women are doing more because they are either contributing to alleviating financial pressure or because their partners are absent for whatever reason - work to meet financial pressures, drugs, alcohol, depression or anxiety.

Even for the stay at home mum there is still an increasing social stigma and an accompanying fear that 'just being a mum' may not be good enough and perhaps makes her less of a modern woman.

The modern day image of a woman and what she should be doing to be worthy is often a big contributor to postnatal depression and lost identity. Many women don't know how to be a stay at home parent without the world of their careers and achievements validating her worth. Many worry they are not doing the job of being a mum well enough.

In relationships before children there may have been an equal division of labour and decisions, but as a child enters the world mums begin to get caught up in their own gender identification war.

She may want to be at home nurturing her child, but financial pressure, attachments to her career identity or an emotionally unavailable or absent partner forces her into the work force.

Some women want to work and enjoy it, but feel guilty because she is not attending to her 'proper' nurturing responsibilities as a mum.

In an attempt to prove her ability as a successful modern day woman, some women can try to micromanage their whole life, including their partner. They take on the leader role of the family in an attempt to create an appropriate balance.

Women do it all, and they do it better, right? So she should be able to prove it.

Only women are starting to feel exhausted and resentful that they have to do it all. What they don't realise is their beliefs about societal roles are contributing to the set-up of this dynamic.

Another scenario is the mum who isn't coping with the demands of work and home. Perhaps she doesn't feel organised enough or capable of the 'I can do it all' persona and is struggling to be there enough for her children while she is at work, or struggling with being able to pursue her personal endeavours because she feels guilty being away from the family. She is tormented by her own moral tug of war.

There is also a lot of competition amongst mothers these days. The message among her peers (which thankfully is starting to shift) seems to be if she has the smartest, best looking, best behaved and fastest developing children then she is doing a good job. If not, it must be because of her shortcomings.

Whether she is working or not these expectations are heavily attached to her worth as a mother, with marginal room for error.

As a result of this pressure depression is taking over for women too – sometimes even making women turn to alcohol, drugs or some other outlet to forget the pain of their perceived life failings.

Women will often swing between depression and anxiety as well. Once they have spent some time feeling like a failure and not coping, wanting to give up on it all, her indoctrinated mindset to "be competent" kicks in again and she starts to set more goals to get back on track. Except she does this with the same belief that *doing it all* defines her worth as a woman. She slips back into anxiety again, trying to control everything and prevent anything from going wrong.

Her exhaustion, resentment, inner conflicts and constant state of guilt are making her feel inadequate too.

She tries to talk about her problems with her partner to feel better, or to make sense of what she's feeling. However he hears her pain, doesn't understand her and goes into fix it mode in an attempt to make her feel better. He may even interpret her communication as being critical or blaming him.

It's important to understand neither partner is doing anything wrong or malicious. She is trying to reach out to her man because she loves him and feels safe to share her innermost feelings and he is trying to fix her to show her his love and make her happy.

However, without this understanding it is too easy to 'evaluate' the conversation with a completely different lens and thus 'respond' in hurtful ways – sometimes not even knowing that you are.

Most women know when they need help. She knows when the pressure is becoming too much. Because women are talkers they are very perceptive about understanding what is happening for her, so she knows what she needs.

At a core level, she knows a woman should be nurtured and cared for by her man. She knows he should be the protector and the provider and he should look after her. It is the way it's always been. We want them to love us. We need them to love us.

However, I'm beginning to suspect a lot of women don't know how to let men love her. When you look at our female role models it is likely you will see we've never really been taught how to be vulnerable to our partners. Even that word vulnerable can make many women squirm.

Women's liberation and the role change of women was only really getting started in our mother's generation and so we have been brought up with a lot of fear around allowing a man to love and nurture us without falling back into a submissive role.

As Eggerich said: *"The problem many women have today…is that they want to be treated like a princess, but deep down they resist treating their husbands like the king."*

Today's woman has grown up fighting for her rights to equality and it's possible we are still fighting with our partner for those same rights, unknowingly shooting ourselves in the foot. Is it possible that we are starting to become the bullies with our nagging, criticising and micromanaging of our partners?

What many women don't realise is we are not approaching the situation in a way that allows him to help us or love us. We try to control how he loves us and try to make him love us as a woman would love one another.

We try to lay it all out on the table the only way we know how - by talking. We tell our partners how we feel, what we think they are doing wrong and what they need to do differently.

What they hear is that you aren't happy, they are at fault and you are telling them what to do because they clearly can't be trusted to know how to fix this themselves. In that one conversation you have unknowingly insulted every facet of what he prides himself on as a competent, successful man. He feels completely disrespected.

Of course, he probably won't be able to articulate this because men seldom think on this level, but I have seen it time and time again with my clients and in my own relationship.

Women sometimes get so caught up in our own obligations, demands and pressures to do it all, tend to everyone's needs and get life right, that we don't even realise we are treating our man with a lack of respect. In a lot of cases it's not intentional.

I believe the demise of love for a woman is coming from a male's uncertainty about his own place in the relationship and because he's often feeling like he needs to defend himself or assert his masculinity.

Both sexes, however, can get what they want, if they both recognised what each other needed and started to give that to each other.

BLACK, WHITE AND GREY

I realise these ideas may be highly controversial and respect that much of this is open to criticism and debate.

So with that said, here is my disclaimer. Not all people fit into these boxes because nothing is ever black and white.

Times are changing. That's why books like this are being read by both sexes.

Men are starting to wake up and realise they need to change and work on their issues with their masculinity. They are talking more and reconciling their past - hence the drop in suicide over the last decade.

A large majority of men who are reading this very book are doing this, so I am no way wanting to paint a picture of men being weak, hopeless and waiting for the heroic acts of a woman to save them. That would be incredibly condescending (and incidentally adding to the men are incompetent persona).

Men are just as capable as women. We need men in our lives. Both sexes have equal merit in life and we need to find a healthy equilibrium so we are all living in harmony together.

Similarly, women are starting to realise they need help and that the way they've been asking for it is not working either. Women are tired and are realising they need to stop trying to do it all, and they too are searching for ways to realign with their partners and stop the *'I hurt you because you hurt me'* cycle.

WHO IS TO BLAME FOR THE DYSFUNCTION OF RELATIONSHIPS?

Although it may sound like it (and I hope it doesn't) I have not turned against my own sex. I do not wish to portray all men as being lost and broken, nor do I wish to portray women as being brow beating, power hungry bullies.

I simply think the natural progression of fighting for women's rights in combination with other societal pressures has created a society of women trying to do it all and take on too much. In the process of fighting for more power women have either forgotten that relationships are a team effort or are struggling to learn how to communicate effectively with their partners without fighting for their needs. They've grown up with their mothers having to fight for their place and are likely to be still using the same tactics.

We already have our equal rights, what we need to establish now is equal treatment of love and respect towards each other – from men and women.

I believe many women have no idea they are causing their man to feel even more insecure. I believe that many women have no idea that respecting their partners more will bring them more of what they are after – love.

This missing link is vital.

Women are nurturers and carers. We naturally want to give love and affection and support our partners, but it's possible we don't understand that this is not the primary love language men operate from. He still values love, but respect is his primary need.

On the other side of the coin, I believe often men don't know how to be an equal party in their homes or know when it's okay to take charge. They are often defending their right to have an opinion or have given up trying and are just in survival mode.

One minute women are portraying that they want to be protected, loved and nurtured and the next she is asserting her right for equality.

For example, here is a post I found on a relationship forum on a topic titled: Man as head of the relationship?

A female poster writes:

The situations I would find it useful are in the areas of physical peril. If we are out somewhere, I would look to him to see to our physical safety. Should we leave? Are we safe? The situations it would not work for me are the day to day decisions that everyone takes turns with. What to eat, which restaurant, when should we buy a new TV? Or large life decisions, like where to live, when to move, when to quit a job? These situations need input from both.

This weekend we went camping and it rained. At one point it looked like the tent might blow away, so we stood in the rain holding it. He marvelled later that I never complained and handled it all so well. I thought about it later and firstly, I wanted to go camping, so getting dirty and wet was expected. Secondly, I figured he wouldn't let us get hurt out there. I trusted that he would say, ok let's just go home, if it got bad enough.

From hours of research and looking into the relationships of many different people, it seems a lot of men are clueless about what is the right thing to do. He's receiving mixed messages because she's giving him mixed messages. A lot of the time men don't know what women want because women don't know what they want!

Just like women have not really had the role models to show them how to deal with this relatively new gender shift into equality, men too have lacked the teachings of how to communicate effectively with his partner and establish a healthy and happy alignment with her.

Men are either just giving in to the 'she's the boss' mentality letting her run the show, disengaging from her and the family in exchange for activities to forget his problems, or asserting his place with aggression and anger.

In all three cases he is adding to her exhaustion and frustrations due to the lack of help.

> **The end result is that men don't feel needed or respected and women don't feel loved. BOTH sexes are part of the problem and thus part of the solution.**

FINDING AN EQUILIBRIUM

Women have come a long way in the world and have earned a lot of respect from men in regards to their capabilities. I think men know women are capable and want to rely on her skills and abilities in the family, but not at the expense of their own feelings of worth.

At one end of the spectrum I think men are tired of the game of women fighting for their rights and are ready to just establish some clear boundaries so they know what to do and how to make women happy.

On the other end, I have seen and heard of many cases where men will seek out the modern day strength in a woman because their partner isn't that way, so I don't believe mean really want subservient, meek wives either.

What they do want however, is something in the middle where they still feel respected and needed.

I believe women still love the idea of having a hero and protector and someone to look after her. It's how she feels loved. It's why the majority of women swoon over action heroes who would do anything in the name of love, or why women get angry at other women who neglect husbands who are clearly devoted to their wives.

She wants to be nurtured, cherished and loved, except she doesn't want this in a way that makes her submissive. She likes her modern day strengths and abilities and wants to be acknowledged and validated for her input. She wants to feel heard and understood and to feel like her opinions and views matter. It's what women have been fighting for, for years.

But now it's time to stop fighting and just start listening to each other's wants and needs. It's time to start communicating, negotiating and forming an alignment between the two sexes. Women have their equal rights. We don't need to keep asserting our rights. Men get it. It's now time to find an equilibrium with these equal rights now, where both parties are feeling worthy and validated in their relationship roles.

There needs to be a BIG shake up in how we are relating to one another because not only is this effecting us, it is also teaching our children the very same way of relating to the opposite sex, these destructive ways of living and potentially setting them up for unhappiness in their relationships too.

We need to realise both sexes are looking for the same thing! Both sexes are looking for validation, approval, acceptance, respect and to feel worthy. Both sexes are looking for pleasure and to avoid pain. Both sexes are asking the question – "What's in it for me?"

Your partner is not the enemy.

In an ideal world it would be great if both partners were reading this book and seeking out information about how to change, but often it is only one partner reading it. That's okay, because change has to start somewhere.

Someone has to do something different to break the cycle. With a clear understanding of what's going on for your partner and making a conscious effort to change your side of things, you are likely to find your partner's attitude and approach changes too.

In his book *Love and Respect*, Eggerich presents many letters and testimonials from his seminars and books where couples have experienced enormous changes just by one of the partners applying this fundamental rule – to give men respect, or to love their woman more.

Co-incidentally I witnessed this transformation from a client I've been working with. This dad came to me for help with being more engaging with his family and to work on his impatient, angry responses. Essentially he wanted to become a better dad and role model to his children.

As our sessions continued our conversations have naturally gravitated towards his relationship with his wife.

Having four children things were quite chaotic and their relationship was at times feisty and hurtful.

What I had not realised until after reading Eggerich's book and understanding the love and respect aspect of what men and women want was that I was naturally teaching him how to communicate with his wife in a way to show her he loved her and understood her. In return she began to naturally show him more respect.

I was ecstatic to see evidence of the very thing I was reading about happening right before my eyes.

Reading all of the examples from Emerson's book of women and men who were both applying this concept to their partners, I knew I had to include this concept in this book and explain to you how to give more respect to your man or more love to your woman.

Chapter Four

UNDERSTANDING YOUR PARTNER'S VIEWS ON LIFE

Gender trends are a generalised way of looking at things and don't address what's going on for all couples.

While I urge you to take the last chapter on gender differences into serious consideration when looking at the potential causes for your present problems, I also urge you to think about your relationship as an individual one, with two individuals looking at life through their unique and equally individual belief systems.

Whether you agree with the gender stereotyping presented in the last chapter or not the reality is that what drives your partner's behaviour is the way they evaluate their life. If you want to change how you "respond' to each other you must understand how you and your partner are thinking.

To do this you need to appreciate the power of your partner's parental and social conditioning and how this has influenced how your partner (and you) perceive life and consequently how this causes you to both behave.

Remember we are all out to seek pleasure and avoid pain and we all have beliefs about a 'right' way to live to be worthy. If in your *'women are from Venus'* way you are unknowingly criticising your man's identity or trying to interfere with his 'right life' this can cause conflict.

Equally, if your woman is discussing a problem that's important to her due to her 'right' life and self-worth beliefs and in your *'men are from Mars'* way you unknowingly dismiss what she's saying, don't take the time to understand, or go into fix it mode then this can also cause conflict.

When you gain a better understanding of the pattern of thinking that lies behind you and your partner and recognise how that thinking has been set up, you may find you have a lot more compassion to work with as you can see where they have attached their self-worth and why certain things are so important to them.

Often when you are in conflict with another person you are only seeing your side of the story. You are only seeing the situation through your lens of perception and how the situation is impacting on your self-worth or right life. Getting a better understanding of the way your partner perceives life and the pattern of their thinking may help you to understand their behaviour and consequently help you to see a pathway to negotiation and compromise. This is something we'll discuss in depth later.

I once worked with a couple who were on the brink of separating due to an emotional affair, but they decided to try and work things out first.

Both of them were depression and anxiety sufferers, so the first thing we did was to sit down with both of them and conduct a questionnaire I usually do with my one-on-one clients.

This questionnaire helps me to ascertain what specific beliefs are behind my clients' stress/behaviour and where these beliefs came from. I asked the questions and one or the other partner became the scribe. It was so valuable for each partner to see the pattern of thinking behind why their other half behaved and felt the way they did and how these beliefs were all set up.

It gave them a new understanding and appreciation for what the other person was going through and those conditional self-worth beliefs their partner had to contend with on a daily basis, which were causing both of them so much pain.

By realising what was happening for the other person they became a lot more encouraging to one another, trying to help them to correct their thinking. They became more understanding of the thinking behind each other's behaviours and weren't so quick to personalise their partner's behaviour.

They both got an understanding of the beliefs that drove the affair to occur in the first place (affairs always occur because of a self-worth belief) and with this new understanding of each other they could begin to repair the damage.

Doing this questionnaire was by no means the only thing that needed to happen in order to put their relationship back together, but it made them a lot more real about the problem, more compassionate and understanding of each other, and gave them a new way of viewing the other person's behaviour (rather than being so quick to react to it).

Getting a deeper understanding of your partner's mental approach to life can explain much about your partner's behaviour.

Your first exercise in this book will be for you to do just that. The following exercise is split into three parts.

If you feel you have quite an open and trusting relationship, you may feel comfortable to complete Part A together, being each other's scribe. Once you have completed Part A, do Part B on each other's questionnaire because you will be more objective about it.

Another option may be for both of you to do Part A on your own, then swap and have each other read Part A and complete Part B based on their answers.

If your partner will not participate in either of these options, then you do Part A and B for yourself and use the questions in Part C to try and gain an understanding of what could be happening for your partner.

Exercise One

UNDERSTANDING YOURSELF AND YOUR PARTNER

PART A

Instructions: Complete the following questionnaire. You can do this as a couple where your partner is the scribe (make sure you feel safe to answer the questions with complete honesty and no reservations) or if you are more comfortable, fill in the questionnaire separately and share your answers when completing Part B.

If you are not doing this with your partner, complete Part A and B on your own, or get a trusted friend to be your scribe and ask you the questions for Part A and get them and you to do Part B together. Then complete Part C.

SECTION ONE: YOUR CHILDHOOD FAMILY

1. How would you describe your family (from childhood) – siblings, parents etc.?

   _____
   _____

2. How would you describe your interactions with each other?

   _____
   _____

3. Were there many conflicts in the family and how were they handled?

   _____
   _____

4. Was there an event from your childhood that you still remember often (good or bad)?

   _____
   _____

5. What was your role in the family?
   What did that role require you to do?
   (Note - everyone has a specific role they played such as the youngest, smartest, prettiest, black sheep, peacekeeper ...)

   _____
   _____

6. Are you still playing that role today?

   _____
   _____

7. Was religion a part of your life?
   a. If yes which one?
   b. Does it have a part in your life today and how?

   _____
   _____

8. What is your family's cultural back ground? Does this and has this affected your life? If so, how?

　　_____

　　_____

Section Two - Yourself

1. **How would you describe yourself?**

   _____

   _____

2. **What are some of the specific beliefs you remember being taught about:**

   You: _____

   _____

   Family: _____

   _____

   Women: _____

   _____

   Men: _____

   _____

   Children: _____

   _____

UNDERSTANDING YOUR PARTNER'S VIEWS ON LIFE

Achievements: _____

_____

Money: _____

_____

Marriages/Relationship: _____

_____

3. **What are the issues you think really cause your stress?**

_____

_____

4. **Do you think your life is going wrong? Why or why not?**

_____

_____

5. **Are you happy with your life right now? Why or why not?**

_____

_____

6. **What is needed in order to fix your life or make it better?**

_____

_____

7. Why can't you accept your life right now?

   _____

   _____

8. What aspect of yourself do you hold in high regard (that is – what do you like about yourself?)

   _____

   _____

9. What aspects of yourself do you hold in low regard (that is - what don't you like about yourself)?

   _____

   _____

Section Three - Your Mother

(or female primary caregiver. If your mother was absent during your childhood please proceed with the questions as you will still hold beliefs about your mother. If you had both a mother who was absent and another primary female caregiver, please complete the questionnaire for each person.)

1. **Describe your mother**

   _____

   _____

2. **What do you think she liked about herself?**

   _____

   _____

3. **What do you think she liked about you?**

   _____

   _____

4. **What do you think she disliked about herself?**

   _____

   _____

5. **What do you think she needed in order for her life to be successful?**

   _____

   _____

6. What do you think she felt you needed in order for your life to be successful?

    _____

    _____

7. Was there an event that occurred as a child between your mother and yourself that still impacts you today?

    _____

    _____

8. Name two lessons you learnt from your mum?
    a. What you would use today?

    _____

    _____

    b. What you wouldn't use today?

    _____

    _____

SECTION FOUR - YOUR FATHER

(or male primary caregiver. If your father was absent during your childhood please proceed with the questions as you will still hold beliefs about your father. If you had both a father who was absent and another primary male caregiver, please complete the questionnaire for each person.)

1. **Describe your father**

   _____

   _____

2. **What do you think he liked about himself?**

   _____

   _____

3. **What do you think he liked about you?**

   _____

   _____

4. **What do you think he disliked about himself?**

   _____

   _____

5. **What do you think he needed in order for his life to be successful?**

   _____

   _____

6. **What do you think he felt you needed in order for your life to be successful?**

   _____

   _____

7. **Was there an event that occurred as a child between your father and yourself that still impacts you today?**

   _____

   _____

8. **Name two lessons you learnt from your father?**
   a. **What you would use today?**

   _____

   _____

   b. **What you wouldn't use today?**

   _____

   _____

Part B

Instructions: Using your partner's questionnaire (or yours if you are doing it without your partner) answer the following questions to help ascertain the pattern of thinking.

If you have a friend helping you then get them to answer these questions with you.

This pattern of thinking will help you to see what the person believes they need to live up to in order to be worthy. This could be an idea of a right way to live (or avoiding a wrong way), an identity, a role they feel they need to play, or repetitive opinions about themselves or others.

This pattern of thinking might also be a habitual view of life. For example, an attitude that it's always someone else's fault may have been taught by dad because he used to think that way.

1. **Are there any repetitive words you used within your questionnaire?**

   _____

   _____

2. **Were there any repetitive themes?** (For example, I kept referring to ideas around achievement, or I found that I kept saying I should be doing more to stop something.)

   _____

   _____

3. Can you see any similarities between one of your parents and your own character and behaviours?

   _____

   _____

4. Was there something you needed to do in order to win the approval of your parents or to feel accepted, loved, important, approved of, or good enough in the eyes of one or both of your parents?

   _____

   _____

5. Did you observe a sibling experiencing emotional pain due to a certain behaviour and you become the opposite of that siblings' behaviour (a subconscious approach to avoiding emotional pain)?

   _____

   _____

6. Were there any ideas about how a life 'should' be lived and/or how yours is going wrong?

   _____

   _____

From your answers to this questionnaire,
can you see where you have attached your identity to your self-worth?

What have you learnt about yourself from doing this exercise?

Part C

This section is only if you and your partner did not do Part A and B either individually or together and you would like to get some insight into why they are behaving the way they are.

Instructions: Consider the following questions:

Note: Try to fill in what you can and perhaps you might be able to strike up an informal conversation with your partner to try and fill in the blanks. Try to get as much of his/her perception of life as you can and be mindful of what might be your opinion, as opposed to his/her views. Try to be mindful of their specific choice of words because this will show you the pattern of thinking.

1. **What do you know of your partner's childhood? How have you heard him/her describe it?**

   _____

   _____

2. **How did your partner's childhood family interact with one another?**

   _____

   _____

3. **Was there a specific event you've heard your partner talk about from his/her childhood that still effects them today?**

   _____

   _____

4. What do you think his/her role was in the family?

   _____

   _____

5. Was religion or cultural values part of your partner's life? If so, how?

   _____

   _____

6. How do you think your partner would describe him/herself?

   _____

   _____

7. How do you think your partner would describe his/her life? Have they ever voiced if it is going right or wrong? Why have they thought that?

   _____

   _____

8. Do you think your partner is happy with his/her life? Why?

   _____

   _____

9. What does your partner think is needed in order to fix his/her life?

   _____

   _____

10. **What aspects of him/herself do you think your partner is proud of?**

_____

_____

11. **What aspects of him/herself do you think your partner is not proud of?**

_____

_____

12. **What do you think your partner believes about:**

Him/her Self: _____

_____

Family: _____

_____

Women: _____

_____

Men: _____

_____

Children: _____

_____

Achievements: _____

_____

Money: _____

_____

Marriages/Relationship: _____

_____

13. How do you think your partner would describe his/her mother?

_____

_____

14. What do you think your partner's mother thought was important to get her life right?

_____

_____

15. What do you think you partner's mother thought was important for her son/daughter to get right in their life?

_____

_____

16. How do you think your partner would describe his/her father?

　　_____

　　_____

17. What do you think your partner's father thought was important to get his life right?

　　_____

　　_____

18. What do you think you partner's father thought was important for his son/daughter to get right in their life?

　　_____

　　_____

Evaluating the questionnaire:

1. Are there any repetitive words your partner often uses?

   _____

   _____

2. Were there any repetitive themes? (For example, ideas around certain achievements or 'right' or 'wrong' ways to live life, things he/she may be missing out on. Was there a tendency to blame others, or blame themselves? Was there a pattern of viewing life in a particular way or repetitive descriptions he/she would use about themselves or their life?)

   _____

   _____

3. Can you see any similarities between your partner's character and behaviours with one or the other of his/her parents?

   _____

   _____

4. Can you see a pattern of something that your partner needed to do in order to win the approval of his/her parents or to feel accepted, loved, important, approved of, or good enough in the eyes of one or both parents?

   _____

   _____

5. Did your partner observe a sibling experiencing emotional pain due to a certain behaviour and has become the opposite of that siblings' behaviour (a subconscious approach to avoiding emotional pain)?

_____

_____

6. Were there any ideas about how a life 'should' be lived and how it was going wrong?

_____

_____

7. From the answers to this questionnaire and the conversations you've had with your partner, can you see where he/she may be attaching their self-worth to a particular identity, goal or 'right' life path? What have you learnt about your partner from doing this exercise?

_____

_____

The objective of completing this exercise is for you to see that your partner's current behaviour has a lot more going on beneath the surface of what you are experiencing.

Remember, behaviour and emotion are just the end result. The cause of these two responses is the evaluation process that occurred before it. If you can begin to get an understanding of how your partner habitually views life, as well as how you habitually view life, you can begin to see what is really causing the conflict.

When you or your partner feel like your self-worth is in jeopardy, that's when defences come up. If you are saying something that makes your partner feel like his/her life is being judged as worth-less or they feel like you are judging their character, they will react to that.

Knowing more about the standards they rate themselves by and where these come from (childhood) is so helpful in being able to understand their behaviour and later in being able to communicate effectively, negotiate and compromise. You're no longer dealing with just the response (their reaction and their emotions) you are working with their evaluation system and able to communicate what's going on in yours.

That means you are going to be making them feel more validated, heard, acknowledged, approved of, respected and accepted for who they are.

This also means getting an understanding of how you have learnt to attach identities, goals and a 'right life' to your self-worth and insight into why you get so reactive too.

Now before you throw that exercise into the *'I don't have time for that'* bin let me reiterate what an important exercise this can be. Doing this exercise alone can give you a whole new perspective on your partner and can completely change the way you approach them about issues.

Section B

The Reality of Your Current Relationship

Chapter Five

TAKING THE FIRST STEPS TO CHANGE: PERSONAL RESPONSIBILITY

By now I hope you are starting to gain a real understanding as to why your relationship is having issues. Whether your relationship is in big trouble or you are reading this book to gain insight on how to improve certain areas of your relationship, I hope it has become clear that the way both of you participate in the relationship is what is causing the conflict.

This section of the book is about getting honest about the reality of where your relationship is at. This chapter will be your first step in doing that by taking an honest look at your part in the dysfunctional areas of your relationship. It's not about laying blame on you, but rather acknowledging that you have played a part in the present dynamics with your partner and thus your relationship's current status.

People who have worked with me will know that one of my most popular catch phrases is:

All stress is a conflict between belief and reality

Belief is what you are thinking and how you are perceiving life. Reality is what is actually happening. It's important to develop a reality-based perspective of what is happening in your relationship.

When you are in conflict with reality, your mind gets stuck rolling around in stories about…

- How life should be different to what it is,
- How you are missing out on what you are supposed to be experiencing,
- How you or someone else should have acted differently,
- What this unwanted situation now means about you and your life.

When your attention is stuck on this kind of story, you are dwelling on something that either isn't happening or an expected outcome that hasn't eventuated. You are stuck on how you think it should have been, but that's not reality. That's not how it is.

When you're in conflict with reality you begin to experience a stress response. This could be anger, frustration, annoyance, depression, anxiety, sadness, loneliness or any other stress response.

In this state of mind your attention is occupied in this story and you aren't looking for the solutions to changing your current reality.

In this section it is time to accept the reality of your relationship so you can begin to make some changes to it and progress towards the relationship you would like to have.

To begin this process, I'm going to address this section to you only, not something for you and your partner to do together.

The reality is a relationship is made up of two individuals with two unique and different belief systems (ways of viewing life and self-worth). Both of you have contributed your belief systems, created emotional responses and reacted to your perception of each other. Both of you have contributed to the problem.

HOW YOUR BELIEFS COULD BE CONTRIBUTING TO YOUR MARITAL PROBLEMS

We have discussed in some detail how we have learnt to attach our self-worth to certain conditions – a right way to live or an identity we feel we must live up to.

In the first section of this book you began to identify some of the patterns of thinking in yourself and got some insights into how they were set up that way.

I could probably write another ten books going through the endless sea of beliefs that may be contributing to the dysfunctional areas of your relationship, so it is more of a self-reflection exercise for you to start looking for clues that link the ways your beliefs are conflicting with your partner's beliefs to create conflict.

Below is a list, which is by no means exhaustive, to give you an idea of how some of your beliefs could be causing conflict in your relationship.

ACHIEVEMENT IDENTITY

- Putting pressure on yourself to get things to be perfect and expecting your partner to know what you need or how to do things your way.
- Getting upset when life goes differently to your expectations and taking it out on your partner.
- Needing to achieve at whatever cost, resulting in your partner feeling neglected or unimportant.
- Blaming your partner for not getting what you want or being able to achieve what you want.
- Criticising or degrading your partner for not doing something as well as you, or even making yourself feel better about your achievements by putting your partner down.

- Not giving yourself a break because you are trying to be the achiever who does everything perfectly, resulting in you being run down, irritable and snappy at your partner.

- Working yourself to the ground in an attempt to get accolades for achieving in your work environment at the expense of your family life.

- Trying to get parenting right and not allowing yourself room for learning and growth. Being in conflict with the reality that you won't always get parenting right.

THE PEOPLE PLEASER

- Not being able to say no to others and causing disruption to your family life or your partner's plans.

- Doing too much and feeling stressed by the pressure to do everything, causing you to feel irritable, tired and snappy.

- Allowing your partner to treat you poorly or disrespectfully to avoid upsetting him/her.

ATTACHED TO A CERTAIN SOCIAL STATUS

- Putting your achievements before your family to create a standing in the community. Not thinking about their needs as well as your own.

- Spending money on yourself to improve how people perceive you at the expense of family needs.

- Taking on a large financial debt in order to prove yourself as being successful.

- Taking on projects that put the family under pressure because you are trying to be seen in a certain light by others

BELIEF: I NEED TO PROVE I'M BETTER THAN OTHERS
(This may have come from a family fighting for attention.)

- You believe your partner is incompetent in certain areas and you are better than them, thus treating them like they are stupid or inferior to you.
- Putting your partner down in front of the kids or other people.
- Getting frustrated that things aren't getting done as well as you would do them.
- Not taking any time out because you don't think your child will be looked after as well as you look after them.

ATTACHED TO A CERTAIN VIEW OF HOW A FAMILY SHOULD BEHAVE
(For example, they should always be happy, get along, and love each other.)

- Getting stressed or angry whenever conflict arises or whenever you notice you aren't living up to the *Brady Bunch* concept of a family.
- Blaming your partner or lashing out at your children because you feel out of control.
- Getting frustrated when the kids are being kids because you believe they should be behaving in a different way causing everyone to walk on egg shells around you.

ATTACHED TO BEING RIGHT

- Continually making your partner wrong.
- Regularly judging, criticising or ridiculing your partner - either seriously or in jest.
- Not listening to your partner's ideas or opinions.
- Having to do tasks yourself because you need them to be done your way.

BELIEF: I'M NOT GOOD ENOUGH

- Fearing your partner will leave you and acting clingy or jealous.
- Relying on your partner to make you feel good about yourself and then feeling hurt and angry when they don't.
- Not wanting your partner to try new ventures or go out without you for fear they will leave you.
- Not wanting to pursue your own interests and relying on your partner for constant stimulation and entertainment.

ATTACHED TO THE MARTYR IDENTITY

- Finding evidence of how you do everything and your partner does nothing in an attempt to gain notoriety for what you do.
- Criticising your partner for not contributing as much as you.
- Doing everything yourself and not asking for help.
- Expecting your partner to automatically know what you need help with and how to do it, then getting annoyed at them when they don't do it.
- Expecting your partner to know when you need time out.

LOOKING THROUGH THE LENS OF 'IT'S ALL ABOUT ME'

- Only looking at what you're not getting and not seeing what's happening for your partner.
- Depriving your partner of wants and needs because you are resentful that your needs aren't being met.
- Not being interested in your partner's life because you are so involved in your own.
- Only focussing on how bad things are for you.
- Asserting your own standpoint in regards to the conflict but not taking the time to understand or respect your partner's standpoint.

To get a clearer view of how your beliefs may be contributing to your relationship, try the following self-reflection exercise:

Exercise Two

SELF-REFLECTION: HOW IS YOUR VIEW OF LIFE AFFECTING YOUR RELATIONSHIP?

1. Reflect on the pattern of thinking and the self-worth beliefs you discovered in Exercise One's questionnaire? What identities or right life did you feel you needed to live up to?

2. Do you think these attachments are contributing negatively to your relationships?

3. Do you have high expectations of your partner because you are attached to getting life right in a particular way? Do you criticise your partner when they don't match that expectation?

4. Do you communicate to your partner in a way they may feel disrespected or unloved because of your attachments to your identity or 'right life'?

5. Do you ever blame your partner for your unhappiness or project your unhappiness onto your partner because of your self-worth issues or fears you aren't getting life right?

These questions are to start you reflecting upon how you treat your partner and how your beliefs are responsible for the way you are treating them.

UNDERSTANDING HOW YOU THINK

The best way to experience peace in any area of your life is to get a greater understanding of yourself and how you think about life. It can be difficult to be candid about your contribution to a relationship issue. It's much easier to blame other people for your problems. You can't change another person's behaviour, but you can change your own. When you get real about your part in the relationship and change that, you might find your partner starts to change their behaviour too.

Happiness begins with self-acceptance and being able to feel comfortable with life's ups and downs. Spending more time on your own personal development will automatically flow onto the relationships you have around you.

I have experienced first-hand the benefits this has to a relationship. By understanding yourself and taking responsibility for your part in the dynamics of a relationship you can achieve much more depth and meaning in your relationships.

I remember in my early years with Steve, before children, when I had wanted to go overseas to do a personal development course. I had just been over to the US for another course and I really wanted to do their next level course. I knew it would be a mission getting Steve to align to this because of the money it would cost to go again.

As we were talking about it I could see it was quickly escalating into an argument. I had been doing a lot of personal development work on relationships and understanding the thinking behind mine and other people's behaviours and I began to look at what thinking might have been behind Steve's reaction to me going overseas again.

Although money was a part of his resistance, it dawned on me he had nothing exciting going on in his life so it was difficult for him to be excited and supportive of what was going on in my life. He was doing a job he didn't like and was seeing his money being spent on everything else with none left for improving his quality of life.

With that understanding I felt compassionate for him and redirected the conversation away from what I wanted and started talking about what he wanted in life. By the end of that conversation we had decided he would leave his job and study to be a massage therapist.

We rearranged our finances so he could do his massage course and I could go on my trip and the decision didn't end up being a fight for what I wanted.

If I had not understood what was going on for him during that initial conversation it would have undoubtedly ended in conflict. This is just one example of many I could share with you how understanding myself and working on my personal development has overflowed into a shift in how I relate to my husband, and also others around me.

All of my relationships are so much better because I have stopped playing the games that came from my incorrect perceptions of life and self-worth.

To 'know thyself' means you have an experiential grasp of what could be happening for the other person and helps you to understand that everyone experiences hopes, fears, dreams, insecurities, strengths and weaknesses. To get real with yourself helps you to create the space for other people to get real too.

Exercise two was the first step towards you getting real with how your beliefs are contributing to the relationship.

YOU TEACH PEOPLE HOW TO TREAT YOU

Your beliefs not only contribute to how you treat other people, but they also contribute to the behaviour you accept from other people.

Your beliefs will set the standard of what is acceptable treatment and what is not.

"You teach people how to treat you" is a phrase I first heard on the famous Dr Phil show. It refers to how you have participated in the set-up of how you are treated and the boundaries you have created between you and your partner.

Remember back to how we learn as human beings - through observation, self-experience and being convinced by others.

At the beginning of your relationship your partner observed your behaviours, experienced your reaction to the way he or she behaved and together you established the terms for the relationship. With the repetition of this information and the conviction of which you held them, your partner has learnt the terms upon which you were willing to accept the relationship.

This happened by voicing your disapproval and intolerance, accepting certain treatment from your partner or rejecting other forms of treatment. You taught them what you considered respectful and acceptable, and what you did not. You taught through repetition and communicating in various ways what you will jump up and down about and what you will be nonchalant about.

You gave your partner a reference point from his past experience of your reactions that determines what he will and won't do again in the future.

Somewhere along the line you have taught your partner that it's okay to interact with you the way that he or she currently does - good or bad.

Over the years people change. We get older, wiser and often more confident in ourselves. We realise we want different things out of life and with that comes the realisation we deserve to be treated differently. Conflict often occurs when this realisation comes into play and you start asserting to your partner that they should be treating you differently. However, because you've not communicated your new relationship terms to your partner they become confused and often defensive.

From their perspective they've always treated you this way - why all of a sudden are you up in arms about what they are doing?

If you want things to change you need to have a deliberate conversation about it. Acknowledge how it has been in the past, but explain that you want it to change and why. That way your partner is clear about the change and understands if you react to his or her old ways.

This is where communication, negotiation and compromise comes in.

Clients and female friends often complain their husbands don't help out enough, or that their husband's lives didn't seem to change at all with the arrival of their children. Often they don't realise that they actually contributed to the set-up of this dynamic.

A friend of mine gripes that her husband works long hours all week then comes home and does nothing all weekend. He's off doing leisure things, leaving her to look after the children. She feels she rarely gets time out.

When she does get time out she has to almost beg for it and is met with a negative attitude about having to look after the kids while she is away, which makes her feel guilty about it.

What she doesn't realise is how easily this dynamic can be set up. Somewhere along the line it had been okay for him to behave like this without her getting upset. However, now she has new information and is upset. He doesn't understand and is getting defensive about her reactions to his behaviour.

Let me show you how easily this dynamic can be set up with a typical scenario I often see when a couple become parents for the first time. This is an excerpt from my book, *The Happy Mum Handbook*:

When the baby arrives, the mother usually handles most of the baby's needs. She feeds the baby the most, she gets up in the night because her partner usually goes to work, she looks after the baby all day, and she gets so good at the role of being the baby's mother that it becomes unspoken that the mother will attend to most of the baby's needs.

When a baby arrives, the mother can often push Dad away to a degree, fearing that he won't do things properly or that he won't know how to do something. She might even do everything herself because it's quicker for her to do it or just because she is so used to doing everything for the child that it becomes an automatic reaction to just do it, without thinking about giving her partner a turn.

Her partner might initially try to help, but is met with criticism that he is not doing it correctly and mum then takes over anyway – or she is already up and doing it before he gets a chance to.

So the dynamic has already started.

You have already started to teach your partner that he is not needed and that you have got it covered. So he begins to stop trying to help and just lets you handle it like you seemingly want to, because you have taught him this.

Because you have it covered, he thinks that you will be fine and off he goes to do other things that maybe he likes to do.

Now, the first few times he does this you might feel happy for him to go out and have some fun. After all, he works hard and deserves a break, and you are quite happy to be at home with your baby and show him or her off to your friends anyway, so you don't really mind him doing his 'guy stuff', thus adding another link to the dynamic.

In contrast, sometimes the case is that your partner never really did anything from the beginning. Maybe he believes it is the woman's job, or he was too scared to try, and because you didn't encourage him or challenge the point, he didn't bother trying to do much and that's the way this dynamic was set up.

Either way, you can see how the circumstances have naturally evolved to an 'unhelpful' partner. It's not that he's inconsiderate; it's more that he's been taught by you not to have to consider that you might need his help a lot. You taught him that you've got it covered.

If the case is that he believes that this is a woman's job and he shouldn't have to do anything, then he believes that you accept and respect his belief, and therefore he doesn't need to change anything because you haven't voiced otherwise.

So now you have a partner who is just doing what has been indirectly agreed to by both of you. He's living his life interacting with you the way that you have taught him is acceptable by you and – incidentally – the way he has taught you to interact with him.

Meanwhile, you are sitting at home with your kids with this building resentment towards his freedom and your lack of it. He comes home from his little outing, all happy and refreshed and is suddenly confronted with a cranky, irritable wife who is snapping or giving him the cold shoulder, and he has absolutely no idea why.

He asks, 'What's wrong with you?' Mortified by a question where you think the answer is blatantly obvious, you blurt out how selfish he is and how he never helps you do anything, and how he's constantly running off doing this, that and the other and leaving you stuck at home, never getting any time to yourself ... and so on.

Your partner has no idea what has just hit him. The name calling gets his back up, he gets defensive, fights back, thinks you're just being a whingeing wife, or that your hormones are acting up and storms off, leaving both of you feeling bad. Or, he begins to help you out of obligation and starts to simmer in his own resentment and anger towards what you've just said.

The truth is, he has no understanding whatsoever of what just happened, and is trying to figure out what is so wrong with him going out and leaving you at home with the baby.

He doesn't understand because you taught him that this was okay, and all of a sudden you come out of the blue with indirect accusations about his character and how bad a father and a husband he is. If you can see it from this perspective, how do you think he's going to react to your seemingly sudden outburst?

I think this is a key mistake we make as couples. We unknowingly set up a dynamic such as this, become dissatisfied with it and then expect our partners to know we are dissatisfied and change it.

We don't look at the reality that maybe we have contributed to this dynamic in some way - all we are seeing is how our partner is at fault. We are in conflict with reality.

Consider these questions.

- If you are not getting enough help around the house how have you contributed to that being okay?
- If your partner is criticising you a lot in front of other people or your children, when did that start? Did you say anything the first time it happened or the second? Have you let it slide hoping it would change and inadvertently teaching him or her that it was acceptable?
- If your partner is out on the town way too often, how has it come to be that this is acceptable? Did you at some stage show you were okay with that and now you're not?
- If your partner is continually cheating on you did they know that was a deal breaker for you? Have you been clear that this is a deal breaker? Or have you been in denial, hoping he would just change? Do you have another priority for not saying anything that has overridden your priority to say anything about it (for example, fear of the relationship breaking up and changing your current way of life).
- If your partner is not helping you at all around the house or not willing to get a job and you are doing everything, at what point did this become okay for you? Did you progressively make excuses for the situation, hope it would get better, or have you avoided addressing the situation so you don't upset him or her?
- If your partner is dismissing something important to you, did you spend enough time emphasising why this is important to you? Do

they even know it is important to you? Have you shown them your passion or level of commitment?

It's important to remind you again that this section of the book is not about blame. BOTH partners are always at fault with the creation of a dysfunctional relationship, but both partners are not always willing to work together on fixing a relationship.

Often someone has to start it off. That's why I'm addressing this section to you only. I am assuming you are the only one reading this book.

If it is both of you, great! You will both need to look at your contribution to the problem. However if it is just one of you, then that's great too. You will need to accept your part in the problem because once you stop your role in the dynamic, the dynamic CANNOT be the same. It has to change.

Whether that's for the best or not is yet to be seen, but the dynamic will change once you change the parameters of it.

PHYSICAL ABUSE

The concept of *'you teach people how to treat you'* can be difficult to understand when talking about physical abuse, because it can be easily interpreted that I'm insinuating that the victim is at fault. However again I stress this is not about blame. It is about understanding the current dynamics between you and your partner.

I have come to understand the cycle that occurs with violence both from the aggressor and the victim's perspective. The aggressor always has insecurities and feelings of powerlessness. They often have past histories of violence against them, either by a parent or another primary carer, or they have deep seated self-worth issues. Rarely, but sometimes, they simply have indoctrinated beliefs that they have the right to treat their partner this way. Even that in itself is indicative of self-worth issues (the need for having power over someone).

The victim will also have major self-worth issues. They too are likely to have experienced a history of domestic violence and in some way have come to expect this level of treatment. It's not necessarily that this person feels they deserve this treatment, because logically they know they don't. It is more likely this level of treatment has become normal and is aligned with how they are already feeling about themselves. They often believe: *"I am worth-less and look, here's the evidence because he or she thinks so too. That's why they're treating me that way."*

Sometimes victims of ongoing abuse may have started the relationship as a confident person, but slowly their self-worth shuts down from many years of verbal or passive aggressive abuse that has eventually escalated to the physical.

The underlying factor is that the victim of the abuse always has a lowered sense of self-worth that needs to be addressed for the relationship to change, or to give them the courage to leave.

Please understand that I'm not saying all abuse is about self-worth - when you are talking about a child that is a completely different scenario. I am only talking about a relationship between two adults where it is a choice to stay or leave. However, as we'll be discussing shortly, that choice is not always as logical as we may think it is.

On a less serious note, it doesn't matter what the dynamic is between you or your partner, each person has contributed to the set-up of that dynamic.

If there is respect and love in the relationship it is because each party has taught the other that they should respect and love and have taught them how to do it (which is my aim for this book).

However if there is ongoing hurtfulness, criticism, ridicule, lack of support, an imbalance of workload or one person contributing more than the other, then we must remember there are always two people contributing to how that dynamic has come about.

Exercise Three

SELF-REFLECTION:
HOW HAVE YOU TAUGHT YOUR PARTNER TO TREAT YOU?

Think about the problem you are presently having with your partner (or just choose one issue at a time). Reflect on the following:

- Has this always been a problem for you?
- If it has, why have you allowed it to continue for so long? What was in it for you to have their behaviour continue? (Note, there will always be a self-serving priority behind why you've never said anything before or why you let it continue.)
- If it hasn't always been a problem, why is it now? Has something changed for you? Do you have new information about life or your self-worth? Do you have a new relationship ideal or goal? Have you tried to communicate this change with your partner?
- Think back to when your partner began to treat you differently. What did you do to encourage it or what didn't you do to discourage it?
- Look at your childhood and what you've discovered in your questionnaire in the first exercise (page 61). Are your beliefs about self-worth playing a part in how you are teaching your partner to treat you?
- Are your insecurities, paranoias, trust issues or attachments to how you think your life should be (your "right life") contributing to the conflict?
- Have you been avoiding conflict with your partner and been uncomfortable to discuss this problem due to a fear of recreating a situation from your past or your childhood?

- Does the way you communicate and treat your partner contribute to the way they treat you?
  - If female, is his behaviour a result of defending or justifying because of your criticism or disapproval?
  - If male, is her behaviour a result of you continually trying to fix her problems and not allowing her to just talk it out, or not showing her enough love, affection or understanding?

The bottom line is you can't change what you don't acknowledge. Understanding your part in the set-up of how you and your partner treat each other helps you to understand the reality of your relationship.

In this chapter you are just gaining insight into what it is you need to change by figuring out where you went wrong. This is how we learn. This is the only value in looking at your past.

Rolling around in your story of how things should be different or how someone else should have behaved differently is in conflict with reality.

If you want to experience a different relationship then you have to make changes. You can't make changes until you acknowledge the mistakes that have created the present reality.

This section of the book is not about blame. It is about understanding and learning from mistakes. It's about moving on which you will hopefully begin to do with the next chapter.

Chapter Six

LETTING GO OF THE BLAME GAME

"I'm always doing everything. He does nothing. All he ever does is come home from work and does whatever he wants to without any regard for what I might need. He never does any housework. I've been asking him for months to sort out this list of things we need doing and he still hasn't done it. He leaves his stuff all over the house for me to clean up. As for affection, I never get any hugs other than a dig in the ribs and a "how about it" every once in a while. He's so grumpy all of the time. He doesn't spend enough time with the kids. He's not romantic. If he keeps going like this, we are not going to have a relationship. He needs to change his ways, or this relationship is going to go downhill. We'll end up splitting up, all because of his selfish ways."

"She's never happy. It doesn't matter what I do, she's always whingeing about something. She never acknowledges what I do to help her. All she ever sees is what I haven't done. She doesn't realise all the little things that I do around the house, or how much time it takes to take care of the outside. She has no idea how tough my job is and how exhausted I am when I get home. Even when I do try to do more, I never do it right. She'll then complain that I didn't do it properly or do it her way. What's the point? I might as well not even bother helping her if all I'm going to get is criticism. I've had enough of her whingeing at me. I'm better off staying at work so I don't have to listen to it. Better still, stuff her. I'm going to have a beer down the pub."

The brain looks for evidence of what you have your attention on. Sometimes we can get stuck in a particular view of our partner and only see evidence of this viewpoint and nothing else.

A perfect example of this occurred with a client of mine.

We had been working together for quite some time and he had made some massive changes to how much he did for his family. He self-admittedly was not engaging enough in family life for many years and he had started to see the effect it was having on his wife and his children, so he wanted to change it.

He had been working hard on making changes to how he dealt with the children, how much he was doing around the house, changing his angry responses and how considerate he was to what was going on for his wife and how he could help her to be happier. He was what you might call a perfect student. Probably one of the most committed clients I have had.

However, it seemed that his wife still wasn't happy. Although he had changed his approach she still seemed to be nagging him, criticising him and appearing to him as being unsatisfied with his efforts.

Our conversations naturally gravitated towards the state of their relationship and upon further discussions about how she was perceiving the situation, it became clear that her reference points were focussed on his past actions.

She wasn't seeing what he was now doing because her attention was on finding evidence of how he used to be. While he was being a dedicated student, he was also being human and making mistakes along with his progress and that was all she seemed to be focussing on.

Her attention was on the 'deficit' she said he was in because of all the times he hadn't been helping. His wife was looking at him with an old reference point, an old lens of the way he used to be.

Before we realised what was happening he would get offended by her criticisms because she was not acknowledging (respecting) his attempts to make her happier. It was a classic mistake a lot of us women make (I say us because I do it too).

However, understanding that she had her attention stuck on an old reference point, he was no longer offended and was able to communicate with her in a way that drew her attention to the new reality without argument. He was no longer reacting to her behaviour because he understood it.

He still needed her to see that things had changed, but the way he communicated with her was different now. There was no rejection, defensiveness or efforts to prove her wrong, well at least not as often as there used to be.

Once he was able to shift her viewpoint on the present reality and his efforts to change, she then began to acknowledge him, which made him feel better and brought more harmony to the relationship. She actually began to realise that he wanted to change and she began to help him to learn how to handle the kids better. Slowly they are learning to communicate more of their wants and needs without constant bickering and criticisms.

Our brain essentially lives in the past, accessing past opinions, beliefs, memories and experiences. Getting stuck in an old reference point of your partner is something that can easily happen and could be the cause of a lot of your issues.

When you are working on your relationship it is imperative to be able to look at the bigger picture and see what is happening now in your relationship rather than how it used to be. Keeping up to date with how your partner views certain aspects of the relationship and their view of life will help you to stay aligned. The reality is that all of us change over the years and so does our perspective on life. This is why communication is so important, not just when learning to solve an argument, but in general so you are up to date with how your partner thinks and feels about their life.

If you have a lot of judgement on your partner for how they are contributing to the relationship you are likely to be seeing a lot of evidence of this judgement, further reinforcing your belief about them. However, if you were to look for evidence of the flipside, you are likely to find that too.

For example, if you have the view that your partner never does anything around the house, challenge yourself to find evidence of what they do around the house.

If you have a view that your partner is lazy and selfish, challenge yourself to find evidence of when they are motivated and doing things that are unselfish.

Deliberately shifting your viewpoint and searching for evidence can make you see the terms 'always' and 'never' are dramatised ways of looking at a situation that are usually not reflective of reality.

During one of my many discussions about this book with my husband he made a small comment that really impacted me. He said, *"You girls don't realise how many little things a man does for you that goes without recognition."*

I pondered upon this for the next few days and started to search for evidence of what he was saying. Oh my, did I start to see the truth of that statement! Little things were being done all over the place that I had taken for granted and never noticed before. Things to protect me and the kids, or look after us, or to make us happier.

For example, we both walked in from the backyard into the laundry and Steve stopped in the doorway to tap on the wall beside a spider's web that had a hole. The spider came running out of the hole. Confused, I asked him why he had done that. "To see what sort of spider it was".

He was protecting his family. Making sure the spider wasn't dangerous to the kids. Having recognised that acknowledgement of things like this is important to a man, I quickly let him know that I realised this was one of those 'small things' he was talking about and thanked him.

Then, not five minutes later, I was taking a hot chicken out of the oven to see if it was cooked properly and, seeing me struggle, he quickly came to my side to ask if I wanted help. He then proceeded to check the chicken for me and asked me to 'watch out' that the juice didn't spit out at me as he cut into it.

Now I know these are little things we might expect our partners to do for us, but that's just the point. We expect it but don't thank or acknowledge them for doing it, and that's really important to them.

In Chapter Seven we're going to look at specific ways you can give more respect to a man and more love to a woman, but in this chapter, we are continuing on with the theme of you first being able to take responsibility for your part in your relationship's problems and being able to accept the reality of where your relationship is currently at.

We get stuck in the blame game when we hold onto old reference points, looking only for what *isn't* happening rather than seeking out what good things *are* happening.

To repair a relationship you must learn how to let go of that blame game. We need to get rid of the 'I'll hurt you because you hurt me' mentality. Someone has to be the hero of your relationship.

Letting go of blame is just the beginning.

THE REALITY OF NOW

Where are you?

Here.

Here, now. In this present moment.

Are you in the past still? Maybe mentally you are, but that's what we need to change.

Where are you physically?

Right here. It's the only place you ever are. The past does not even exist until you bring it into the present with your mind. Your mind cannot distinguish between what is real and what is vividly imagined. That's why when you focus on a painful past event you can conger up the same emotions you felt back then.

Your thoughts create your emotions.

Now if you are stuck in blame mode over a past event with your partner you are creating those same emotions.

All stress is a conflict between belief and reality. If you have made a commitment to resolving an issue with your partner or repairing your whole relationship this has to be done from the present moment.

There's no point rehashing the past and bringing up past hurts for the sake of blaming. It will only cause further hurt.

The only benefit bringing up the past has, is if you are doing it with the intent to understand it and learn from it.

There's a big difference between telling your partner, *"You did this to me [in the past]. You always do this to me. You don't care about me."* and saying, *"I don't understand what was happening for you back then. Can you tell me so that we can figure out how to avoid doing that to each other in the future?"*

To have a successful relationship you must learn how to let go of the blame over what has been done in the past and focus on how to repair the present with communication, solutions and action.

UNDERSTANDING YOUR PARTNER'S PAST CHOICES AND ACTIONS

Sometimes it is difficult to let go of this tendency to blame when your partner has done something major, or has repetitively behaved in a way that has caused long term resentment.

By now you should have a fairly solid understanding of your partner's habitual evaluation system and where he or she attaches their self-worth. By now you may also have a good understanding of your own evaluation system and how both of you have probably been contributing to the conflict in your current relationship.

Knowing about your partner's upbringing combined with their gender approaches to life it's possible you already have clarity into why your partner behaved the way they did in their past.

However, some of you may still be stuck in the mindset of how they shouldn't have behaved that way or how they should have made a better choice. Perhaps you are stuck in the repetitive story in your mind that your partner knew they shouldn't have behaved that way, but they still did and you just can't let it go.

To 'forgive and forget' requires a deeper understanding of behaviour and the evaluation process.

To begin with I want to dispel the myth that forgiving and forgetting even go hand in hand because they actually don't.

The brain never forgets. It has everything that has ever happened to you stored away in tidy little compartments that link with other compartments. Past events and memories are triggered when something occurs in your present that the brain links as being relevant to something in your past.

When I was a child I used to have a cocker spaniel who only had three legs. She had three legs because of a car accident that occurred when my dad wouldn't let her get in the car because she was dirty. At the tender age of nine, I watched my six month old puppy do somersaults under the car's wheels and can still conger up the same emotion I felt back then watching it happen.

I have forgiven my dad, but every time I see a cocker spaniel my brain recalls that memory. But that's all it recalls - the memory and the event - not any thinking about my dad's involvement in why it happened.

Similarly you may still recall an event that occurred with your partner that caused you hurt. You will never forget it. It will be put away with the rest of your memories until something comes up to trigger it again.

What causes the pain however, is not the memory itself, but what you believe that memory means about you and your life. The pain comes from what issues you are still having with that event and the fact that it occurred.

This is where forgiveness comes in. Forgiveness takes the sting out of the memory.

> **Many people misunderstand what forgiveness is. They interpret it to mean that you are forgiving the act – condoning the act. However forgiveness is not about the act, but about understanding the human behind the act. It's an understanding of why the person did what they did and an acceptance of the reality that they did it and it couldn't have been any other way.**

KNOWING THE DIFFERENCE BETWEEN RIGHT & WRONG, BUT DOING THE WRONG THING ANYWAY

As you know, it is the agenda of all human beings to seek pleasure and avoid pain. It is a primal and instinctual function.

We have learnt how to do this through our experiences of life and the beliefs we have formed. Our habitual beliefs about life are responsible for all of the decisions we make and actions we take.

When someone has acted immorally or hurtfully it is easy to point the finger and *say 'they should have acted differently'*, however this is both in conflict with reality (because the reality is they did do it) and in conflict with the reality of how the brain operates.

Logic is something we are all familiar with. We logically know about morals, values and how to treat people, especially the ones we love. We even have a logical reference point of the person we want to be and how we want to behave to get what we want (pursue pleasure by living the life we want).

However logic is a function of the conscious part of the brain. It is responsible for just five percent of your brains activity. It is like the steering wheel of a car. You consciously try to steer a car in whichever direction you want it to go.

Your habitual thinking is done with the unconscious part of your brain. It is responsible for 95 percent of the brain and you are very rarely conscious of it. In fact you never really choose your beliefs.

At best, you just become conscious of the beliefs as they arise from the subconscious and then you may (or may not) *consciously* act on those thoughts.

The subconscious part of the brain can be likened to a satellite navigation system that makes your car (brain) take over from the manual function (consciousness, logic and reasoning) and automatically self-drive according to its programming (via the subconscious), just like real cars can do these days.

Even though you may logically want to steer your car to go north, the satellite navigation system may have been programmed to head south and it overrides the steering (your logic) at times.

Let's paint an emotionless scenario of how this might work:

If I held up a blue pen to you and ask you what colour it is, your brain is likely to come up with the answer blue.

Did you deliberately select that answer? Or did you only become aware of that answer when it entered the conscious part of your brain that you are aware of (the five percent)?

Were you aware of the brain processing what the words I was saying even meant, determining why I was asking the question, assessing the tone and agenda I may have had for asking the question (was I mocking you or tricking you?).

Were you aware of the brain assessing all of the colours it could have been - green, black, red, blue on the outside but could be red on the inside, and every other colour and combination it needed to compare what it was seeing with past information, beliefs and memories? Then assessing how you should respond to that question - Is it funny? Should I trick her? Should I make a joke of the question?

Then your brain would have been assessing your agenda for answering the question - will I get an approving response or not? And finally assessing how you should physically respond to the question - laugh, get annoyed, use hand gestures or snatch the pen out of my hand for effect? This is where the 'what's in it for me' concept kicks in. What is going to help me to pursue pleasure or prevent pain?

Would you have been aware of any of that evaluation process going on before you gave the answer of blue?

The answer is no, because all of that happened in the subconscious. When the innocent question was posed, the satellite navigation system kicked in with an automated response based on its programming.

This is what is happening in your brain *all of the time.*

Now when we're talking about a simple question about what colour a pen is, there's quite a lot of information to process in one moment isn't there? Yet your brain does that in a split second.

It's also a fairly straight forward and non-threatening situation too. That is of course, unless there is some other programmed information being accessed like an obsessive compulsive condition or paranoia which may cause a different response.

Regardless of the reaction, the evaluation process is the same. Your brain accessed the information it needed to understand the situation and responded to it in accordance with the most appropriate information available in that moment.

This same process occurs with *every* decision you make and action you take.

The most important beliefs activated by the brain in the moment (the priority belief) dictate the response – how a person feels and how they behave.

When someone does something they logically shouldn't have done or they know not to do, it was because the brain accessed a programmed priority belief which dictated their behaviour.

Furthermore their thinking process occurred with the agenda to pursue pleasure and avoid pain *in that moment*. Whether they were logically aware of that thinking or not, there was a story behind their actions that held more weight than the story of logic. The 'what's in it for me' concept kicked in and they determined the pleasure the choice gave or the pain they avoided was ultimately their priority and superseded the pleasure or pain of the logical choice.

Here's another fairly unemotional example of logic versus an act that goes against all logic – smoking.

Logically we all know that smoking is bad for you, yet many still do it. Why? Because of the story smokers tell themselves about smoking.

Smoking is generally about time. Time out for me. *"I'm going to take a break and have a cigarette." "I need some time out." "I've had enough. I need a cigarette."*

The story *'in that moment'* which was accessed by the subconscious included all of the information about the pros and cons of smoking and not smoking that has been stored from past experiences and knowledge.

Even though logical information about why you shouldn't smoke and the detrimental effects on your health were there (which could potentially cause pain), *in that moment* the story about the pleasure the smoker would get from having that cigarette was the stronger priority.

I keep highlighting the words *'in that moment'* because they are key words to understanding priority beliefs. The brain is constantly receiving new information from our experiences and is constantly assessing 'what to do' with the current information presented and how that is linked with past information and experiences.

Often after we have made the decision to do something and have taken action we receive new information (the consequence) and this new information often makes us think we should have acted differently. However, that wasn't the information that was accessed in the moment before the act, was it?

The reality is you have a judging brain and it is always judging what is in your best interests and what will lead you to the most pleasure and avoid the most pain.

It will assess the situation with all of the beliefs, memories and opinions it has gathered from your past and it will access the priority belief most important *'in that moment'* to determine the correct response (behaviour and emotion).

When trying to reconcile with the reality of an unwanted past event we have to be able to see that the event couldn't have happened any other way, because in that moment the priority beliefs accessed dictated the behaviour. The proof it couldn't have been any other way is that it didn't happen any other way. That's the way it was!

Let's pretend for a moment that you could undo the past and change things to be different. To undo the action you would need to get in your time machine and undo every single event that contributed to the set-up of the belief system that created the person's priority belief to be activated in that moment. But we can't just change the act, we also have to change the evaluation process that caused the act to occur. And we need to change all of the situations surrounding the act and all of the beliefs activated by the other people involved in the situation too.

Let's take a situation like cheating for example. To undo this act you would need to jump into your time machine and undo the following:

Starting from the most recent and working backwards to change:

- The day of the act and all of the situations that led to the act on that day.
- All of the people who contributed to the act occurring - the motel attendant, the cab driver that drove them there, the work situation that sent them on that work trip, the bar tender that served them too much alcohol.

- The beliefs of the 'other' person involved in the affair and all of their past events that brought them into your partner's life.
- All of the situations that caused conflict between you and your partner that caused your partner to ultimately choose a new pursuit of pleasure over the logic of being faithful.
- All of your beliefs that contributed to the conflict or to the dynamic of your relationship.
- All of the past events that contributed to your beliefs and all of the past events and beliefs of the people who influenced those events, and thus your beliefs.
- All of your partner's beliefs that contributed to the conflict or the dynamic of your relationship.
- All of the self-worth beliefs set up in your partner and the people and circumstances that influenced those beliefs.

Guess what? You're going to be gone in your time machine for a very long time. You've got a lot of work to do to change the past - it's just not that simple!

This is why we need to let go of what has happened in the past. There is absolutely no point in dwelling on it. The reality is that it happened; it couldn't have been any other way because of all of the events, beliefs, influences and interactions with many other people that occurred leading up to that one act.

If you are now committed to moving on from that past event, repairing your relationship and mending any ongoing resentments between you, you have to do it from a completely fresh perspective.

Rather than dwelling on the act itself, try understanding that person's behaviour and start a dialogue about what was going on in their mind at the time of the event, or as the years progressed if it is an ongoing issue.

Try to hear their perspective. Reflect on your own contribution to the current dynamic or your part in why the event occurred.

It's not about laying blame. It's about accepting the reality that both of you with your unique belief systems came together and produced a result.

We have to let go of the right and wrong aspect and look at it from a cause and effect aspect.

I'm not saying their act wasn't wrong, I'm simply saying you can't dwell on that if your intention is to repair your relationships.

Learn from it and move on is what is needed.

Here are some further examples when considering some of the most common situations where the blame game keeps us stuck from moving forward and how to understand why it has occurred. Remember, understanding is the key. We're not condoning these actions or justifying them, we're investigating the human behind the action and what was going on in their evaluation process to cause this behaviour.

If nothing else, doing this will help you to see that their action was not about your character, but about what was going on for them.

THE CHEATING PARTNER

This is by far one of the biggest difficulties to overcome in repairing a relationship. Logically we all know not to be unfaithful, so why would someone do that to someone they loved?

The answer to this question will be in how your partner was evaluating their life *'in that moment'*. Perhaps they were feeling neglected, unloved, unappreciated or disrespected and found someone who was fulfilling these needs. Perhaps your partner never felt they were good enough and someone else made them feel they were. Perhaps your partner felt like they could never get enough attention from the opposite sex and felt a compulsive need to repetitively get it from multiple partners at once. Perhaps there was a story dating right back to their childhood of using sex as a way of feeling good enough or accepted.

There are so many reasons why a person cheats and it is never about the other person, but rather about what the cheater was feeling about themselves and their life at the time of the event.

When I worked with the couple I mentioned earlier trying to repair their relationship after an emotional affair took place, the questionnaires revealed a deep seated lack of worth in the female partner, which was the source of her cheating. It wasn't because she didn't love and respect her husband.

In fact she knew she had a wonderful husband who was a fantastic father and a very loyal, providing husband. She knew he adored her. It's just she didn't feel good about herself and that caused her to fall for the affections of someone who was giving her fresh attention and making her feel good. Plus there were other beliefs about her life that she was already questioning which had nothing to do with her husband. The grass-is-always-greener allured her to the emotional comfort of another man.

If you are dealing with a cheating situation, communication about what was happening for your partner and how he or she was feeling about themselves, their life and your relationship will be a key factor in repairing the damage.

No progress will be made by rolling around in the fact that it shouldn't have happened and reminding them of how they should have made a different decision. In fact it will only drive you further apart for he or she will continue to feel like they have to constantly defend their actions as you continue to beat them down for them.

There's no love on this pathway and no repairing either. If you have decided to try and move on from this act, then get the information to provide the understanding and move on with repairing the miscommunications that may have caused it so it won't ever happen again.

REPETITIVE VERBAL OR PHYSICAL ABUSE

First and foremost when dealing with this issue the other person must be willing to work on their side. It is unlikely you will be able to do a lot if the other person is not open to seeking help with their anger issues.

I know I've said if you make changes to your side of things, you will see changes in your partner too. However when it comes to anger issues, the problem isn't even about you. You may be their trigger and you can certainly look at that side of things, but you can't be responsible for their behaviour and they need help to address their anger issues for the relationship to improve.

You absolutely must look after the safety of yourself and your children first and then work on the relationship as he or she is getting help too. The giving of more respect and love will still work and go a long way to improving the relationship, but the anger issue itself must also be fixed.

That said, to help you to get an understanding of your partner's anger, the focus needs to be on what that person is really angry about. Where did they learn that behaviour? What is going on for them in their evaluation process to cause this response?

Do they have an expectation of the 'right life' they are supposed to be leading? Are they trying to live up to an expectation or an identity they have come to believe defines their worth? Are they happy with their life?

What is the story they tell themselves when they respond this way to make it okay in their mind?

Also, what has been your participation in this dynamic?

Take a look at your own history. Are there abusive relationships in your past too? Have you unknowingly learnt how to trigger anger, expect it, look for evidence of what is wrong or have you learnt at some level that this sort of treatment is normal? Remember, logic is not largely controlling your evaluation process, decisions or actions.

I broach this aspect very tentatively because without being able to show you evidence of your participation in it, it may be difficult for you to conceive of the idea that your beliefs contribute to this dynamic too.

I am not casting blame on anyone either for the abuse. Morally there is no excuse for abuse of any kind, but morals and values can often be overridden by stronger beliefs about protecting self-worth if it is deemed to be in jeopardy (e.g. she or he is making me feel powerless).

Again, gaining an understanding of what is going on in both partners' minds causing their behaviours will be what will help to resolve this issue.

An honest and candid communication line and a professional mediator and counsellor will be needed to assist this reconciliation. This is a service that we offer at the *Parental Stress Centre*.

AN ABSENT OR DISENGAGED PARTNER

Why has this occurred? What is going on for your partner? Why did they disengage in the first place?

Again, don't dwell on the action, understand the person and their evaluation process behind the action.

I empathise that there may be long term resentment of the work that you may have had to do while your partner was disengaged from you or your family, but if you are serious about reconciling and making your relationship better you must let go of what has happened and focus on why it happened in the first place and how you can change that to create a more harmonious partnership *now*.

When someone has retreated from a situation when they morally should have stuck around it will most likely be because they were protecting themselves from further pain, or pursuing pleasure due to originally perceiving there was a lack of it.

An understanding of their 'story' is needed so you can establish new boundaries, new agreements and find a way to repair the relationship with negotiation and compromise so neither partner feels mistreated, neglected, hurt, bored or uninterested in staying.

Develop an understanding of why they felt the need to disengage or leave instead of staying and talking it out. Have they just never learnt to do that? Have they ever had the role models to teach them adequate communication skills? Are they stuck in gender or parental indoctrinations where they are too proud to ask for help?

New ways of spicing things up, reconnecting, showing and receiving love and spending time together may be needed so your partner doesn't need to become disengaged.

Perhaps your partner needs to reassess his or her own life, goals and direction if they have become depressed by their life.

Find out what they are feeling, try to understand your partner and from here you can begin to create steps to dealing with the real problem – how your partner feels about him/herself – rather than continuing with dealing with their behaviour.

A PARTNER WITH AN ADDICTION

I have spent quite a bit of time in my coaching career helping people with many different kinds of addictions – drinking, drugs and food.

In all addiction cases there is a void in that person's life that the addiction attempts to fill. When dealing with a partner with an addiction, it's important to disassociate their behaviour from your self-worth. It's not because they don't love you or don't respect you.

In fact it has nothing to do with you at all. It's all about what their beliefs are about themselves or their life.

Logically your partner knows they should be more attentive with you and the family. Logically they know they shouldn't take the drugs, alcohol or eat junk food. However, *in the moment* the decision is made to take the substance - a priority belief has been activated that overrides all logic.

Take food for an example. We often resist the temptation of having too much take away or junk food and may cave by saying *"Oh stuff it. I deserve it."* Or *"It's Christmas. That's the time when you can eat whatever you want."*

These statements are common to most people and is a classic case of priority beliefs overriding logic.

With someone with an addiction the same is occurring, but the priority belief will have its roots in a deep seated self-worth belief that almost always comes from the addict's childhood.

They will have learnt in order to be worthy or to feel good enough there is some ability they believe they are supposed to have. This ability will be something they believe they should be able to control.

Because their attention is on the need to have this ability in order to prove their worth, their attention will be on looking for any potential situation that will threaten this ability. With focus on these potential threats they find evidence of their lack of ability and thus feel worth-less – and they therefore continue to find evidence of what is wrong in their life and how they are not worthy because of it.

Drugs and alcohol are an attempt to feel better about themselves *in that moment*. It is an escape from the pain of feeling worth-less. The statement *"Oh stuff it. I deserve it."* runs a lot deeper for those who are addicts.

With any addiction there will be a self-worth story behind it that needs to be addressed and corrected in order for the addiction to be overcome. This will likely need to be addressed before the repairs to the relationship can take place.

It is possible the relationship issues are triggering the addiction – *"I'm not happy in my relationship and the addiction is my escape"*. However, the underlying self-worth belief about what the addict believes the relationship issues means about him or her need to be addressed.

Even if you do repair the relationship, the addiction might stop, but if the underlying belief is not rectified the addiction will likely rear its ugly head again next time the relationship runs into turmoil. Or if another event triggers the same priority belief, the addict will likely resort back to the old reference point of how to deal with it – the substance abuse.

When it comes to food addictions this is usually about food deprivation. They feel their life is being deprived of certain experiences that will make it worthy. They feel dissatisfied, bored or unhappy with their life and the food acts as a substitute for the dissatisfaction.

To deprive themselves of food is depriving themselves even further of a happy life. The *"oh stuff it. I deserve it"* statement also runs much deeper for a food addict.

To repair relationship damage as a result of addictions, just like anger, the other person must be willing to work on themselves personally. It's unlikely long term change will be made just by the other partner making the effort to change.

That said, you can still work on understanding your partner's triggers to wanting the substance and help them to set up situations where those triggers aren't occurring. If you are a trigger, you can certainly work on how you can change yourself so you aren't triggering them. However, you also have to be wary of losing your own personal integrity in the process - more on this later when we deal with the topic of compromise.

Accepting your part in the set-up of your current relationship dynamic

There is no doubt your partner is partially responsible for the conflict in your relationship, but the reality is, so are you.

With any relationship there is the reality of two individuals with two unique belief systems integrating together. How those belief systems integrate will determine the level of harmony or conflict.

Before moving on and changing your relationship you must be able to identify how both of you took part in the problem.

Sometimes this is difficult when dealing with major conflicts like some of the events we just touched on above, but you must accept the reality that in the lead up to this event you were a contributor who influenced the event.

Ultimately it was their decision to act, but your actions also played a part in their actions. In order to repair or improve your relationship, you must take responsibility for your part in it and change that also.

Chapter Seven

PLAYING YOUR PART IN THE SOLUTION

The other day our family had decided we were going to go skiing with some friends. Steve very kindly offered to get up extra early, pack all the lunches and get everything ready. He said all I had to do was get up and get myself ready. Perfect, right? Nothing to complain about there.

However, he woke me up 45 minutes before we were going to leave. The house was a mess, I had nothing to wear and I felt rushed on a Sunday morning when I usually like to get ready at my leisure.

Did I speak of any of this though?

No way. However, in the past I definitely would have griped about all of these things.

Before then I didn't realise that by complaining I would have undermined his good intentions to make me happy. I would have unknowingly disrespected him and came across as being ungrateful.

Now this might seem logical to some of you, but many other women may be making these very same mistakes.

Of course I appreciated what he had done by getting up early and doing everything for our family day out, but consumed in my own world of crankiness I would not really have thought about that. I would have thought my complaining was completely separate to the getting the food and family ready aspect. After all, I wasn't complaining about the food or the packing of the clothes and towels, so I wasn't directly picking on his efforts, right?

However, in his mind I would have been. Because in his mind, what he did was an act to please me and if I showed him I wasn't pleased I have disrespected his efforts.

That said, I didn't feign my happiness either, for I was in a cranky mood. What I did instead was thank him for getting up early and doing everything so I could sleep in. I told him that I appreciated the sleep in and I was grateful for not having to organise everything myself. I then told him I had woken up on the wrong side of the bed and was feeling irritable, without going into the details of why.

That way, he could separate my mood from anything he had done because he knew I still appreciated him.

Rewind into my past and I'm sure the outcome of that morning would have ended up in a very different result – with me being even more irritable and Steve feeling annoyed too.

A second incident occurred about a week later that also changed the way things were discussed. We had arranged a money discussion. This is something I often cringe at because it almost always ends up in an argument and both of us feeling disgruntled about our money situation as well as cranky at each other.

You see our agreement for this year was that I take the time to work on *The Parental Stress Centre* while he worked. It was putting enormous pressure on our finances for me not to have a regular income and for him to have to carry the full load.

Steve is a traditional man and money is hugely important to him. Many men are money driven and attach it to their worth and Steve is no different. We've had many discussions about this, both before and during the lead up to writing this book. It is with this knowledge that I was able to diffuse a potentially nasty conflict.

As we discussed where we were at financially and what we needed to do, it became obvious I may need to go back to paid regular work sooner than we'd planned.

From my side of things that meant giving up on my dream to pursue *The Parental Stress Centre* as I would like to and give up years of hard work in the process. I could feel my desperation to hold onto our original agreement until the end of the year.

On his side of things I could see he was frustrated and discouraged that he was working hard just to cover our living costs and if he didn't keep up his current workload then sometimes we wouldn't even be doing that. On top of this we had a tax debt to pay back that wasn't even getting looked at because all he was doing was covering our living expenses. If we were to get ahead at all I needed to make an income, now.

The other difficulty was that I could go back to work, but it would only be for 10 weeks because then the Christmas school holidays would be upon us and if I was working most of my income would go into school holiday care for our two boys, which was pointless.

While we both agreed there was no point me going back to work until the end of the school holidays (buying me my much needed time) I could see Steve was still very irritated. And rightly so. He's doing a job he hates (he's a painter), he can't afford to hire anyone to make his job easier and to give him some much needed company while he worked, and he wasn't even making any money above paying bills. I could totally understand his annoyance.

On my side of things I was feeling discouraged and guilty that I wasn't getting my business to where I needed it to be quicker, so I was feeling equally irritated.

At the end of the conversation, both of us were irritated. I said something (I can't remember what) and Steve retorted, *"yeah, you're not the one who has to go out to work and earn $xxx each week doing something that you hate."*

Of course that got my back up and usually I would have gotten all fiery and angry at his response but today was different.

Today I could see straight away what was behind his comment. He was really expressing his own unhappiness over not being where he wanted to be in his life. Yes, I was part of the problem, but he wasn't really directing it at me. His comment was about him and what he felt the situation meant for him.

Money is so important to Steve. As a man he prides himself on providing for his family and has always wanted a comfortable financial lifestyle and has worked hard to try and get it. We've made decisions in the past as a couple that have resulted in us struggling for the past few years and it just felt like we were getting further behind because of those past decisions.

All of that was behind that comment. It wasn't aimed to hurt me. It didn't mean he didn't love me. He was frustrated at the situation and was venting at me, not blaming me.

Strangely enough, *in that moment* I could totally see that, and although I was still annoyed at the comment I stood up and said, *"I'm finishing this conversation. We can't go down this road or we'll just end up in a fight. How do you think I'm supposed to feel when you say something like that? I just feel even guiltier than I already do and then I'll react. We just have to stop talking about it for now."*

The conversation ended with no nastiness or bitterness and no giving each other the cold shoulder for the rest of the night, which undoubtedly would've been the result if I hadn't realised the real reason behind his comment.

In the past I would have retaliated with something equally as hurtful.

In hindsight I can still think of better ways to handle that conversation. For example, I could've heard that statement and acknowledged that I understood that it must be very discouraging for him to work so hard and how helpless he must feel being unable to do anything about it. I think appreciating what he does do would have helped in making him feel better about where he was at. This would have acknowledged that this wasn't his fault or a reflection of his failings.

However, in my state of fear over losing years of hard work and late nights and having to let go of a dream I've had for a long time, I wasn't quite at this level of clarity. It was the best I could do *in that moment*. I know the more I apply the information you are reading in this book (and the information to come) I will get better at recognising what's happening for both of us and knowing how to handle situations to avoid arguments and diffuse tense conversations.

So far in this book I have been trying to arm you with an understanding of both why your relationship is where it is, your part in it being that way, and helping you to understand what's going on for your partner.

With this information we can now move into a solution focussed approach to your relationship issues so you can also begin diffusing the tense issues you have or applying these solutions to those little moments like our family day out.

The reality is you can't change the way you interact with each other by rehashing the past and continuing with the same games and behaviour that landed you here in the first place.

As I've said before - you cannot change what you don't acknowledge. When you can acknowledge how you have gotten to where you are you begin to accept your reality.

Accepting your reality doesn't mean you'll like it, nor does it mean that you won't want to do anything about it. However, it does mean that you are ready to face your reality.

It is from here you are can start also looking for solutions to change this reality.

The truth of your relationship is that something has to change. You can't keep doing the same thing and expecting a different outcome.

For men, this will mean making a conscious effort to rise above any situations where she is complaining, criticising, putting you down, appearing to be unhappy, blaming you or just generally acting in a way you perceive as being unappreciative and disrespectful.

For women, you will need to make a conscious effort to rise above situations where you feel he is being hurtful or being cold, dismissive, uninterested, critical, unsupportive or irritable too.

I promise you it won't be for the long term when you begin to apply the methods taught so far, in conjunction with what you learn from here on in.

But this may not be easy at first. You will need to exercise conscious awareness as much as possible, because your habitual thinking will want to return to old habits. This road doesn't lead to change. Conscious effort NOT to respond in your usual ways and to apply a new way of approaching your partner, is what will return you the results you want.

You have to let go of old reference points and focus on right now. You need to commit to your intention to change the relationship for the better.

The art of negotiation is finding a way to get what you want while giving the other person what they want. If a man shows a woman he loves her, he will get more respect. If a woman shows her man she respects him, she will get more love.

Try it and see what difference it makes.

Chapter Eight

FOR WOMEN: WHAT MEN WANT & HOW TO GIVE THEM MORE RESPECT

WHAT DOES RESPECT MEAN TO A MAN?

Look at the history of a man. For thousands of years men have been depicted as strong leaders, but the reality is that gender roles aren't the same as they used to be, at least not in a traditional sense. The challenge now is to find an equilibrium that works for you and your partner because the rules aren't clear anymore.

> **I believe both men and women are very confused about what is the right role for a male to play and the wrong role to play, and every person has a different take on this.**
>
> **It is not for anyone to tell you how it should be, but for you to figure out how you and your partner want it to be.**

This is something I'm going to guide you to be able to do in later chapters. In this chapter we still have to deal with a male's desire to have certain needs met in order to feel good about himself.

Although men may want to succeed in these roles in different ways it is important for women to understand the following attributes are highly important to a man.

This is not just generational gender roles. It's deeply ingrained in his core. He needs this like women need talking to feel supported and understood. Just stop talking about your problems and see how difficult and unnatural it is. That's how unnatural it would be for him to give up any of the following things.

As a general rule, **respect to a male equals appreciation**.

You can show respect to a man by appreciating:

- His **work** ethic or how hard he works;
- How he **protects** his family by doing 'the little things' such as fixing things, stopping potentially dangerous situations and thinking about how to keep his family safe;
- His desire to be the **leader and** a position of **authority**. Ouch! Did I just say the 'A' word? This one may be a little tough for some women, but I'll elaborate on that shortly.
- His desire to **fix your problems** and **be the expert**. Allow him to offer his opinions and advice to you;
- His need for connection through **independence, space and activity**;
- His need for **sexual intimacy**.

Men want to feel like they are needed but not in a 'you're the help that walks through the door' kind of way that can happen when you are a parent.

He wants to know that what he's doing or what he's already done has been needed. He wants the approval and gratitude – the gold stars.

APPRECIATE HIS WORK

I often think women underestimate how important work and achievement is to a man. It is often how he defines his very existence.

Reflect again upon the history of the male species and you will see that working has become the very fabric of who a man is. Being able to achieve and 'bring home the bacon' has become a way that a male defines his worth. It's almost a primal function.

Take a look into his past and what he's learnt about work from his father and his upbringing and you will get an idea of how your partner has been indoctrinated to think about working and achieving.

Even if it seems your partner is not taking his responsibilities seriously, it might not be due to a lack of desire but depression over feeling he has failed in his achievements in the work arena or in another area of life.

If your partner is not working it's likely it will be eating away at his self-esteem and at some level he's not feeling good enough, or perhaps it could be the fear of potentially failing that is stopping him from trying to work.

In rare cases you may find you have a partner who may not be driven in this arena at all - this too is likely due to his male role model influences. Rather than be critical of him for what you perceive are his shortcomings, try encouraging him to pursue his interests and try new things and help him to experience the pleasure in working.

If it is necessary for him to work to help you to meet the family's financial obligations, rather than trying to change him try to inspire him to *want* to work. Help him to focus on his strengths and interests. When you believe in him he is likely to feel better about himself.

When it comes to work you will notice a big response in the way he treats you when you praise, acknowledge and respect his work ethic and trust his ability to provide for the family.

You can do this in very simple ways:
- a. Acknowledge that he gets up every day to go to work.
- b. Acknowledge it if he works long hours.
- c. Does he do something that he hates to provide for the family? Appreciate his efforts to do this.
- d. Does he go to work so you can stay at home with the children? Does he sometimes feel like he misses out on the kids growing up because of his work? Acknowledge that you appreciate this sacrifice.

e. Acknowledge his loyalty to his boss or his work ethic to do a good job.
f. Tell him something you admire about the way he works.
g. If your partner loses his job he will likely feel a little (or a lot) worth-less or bad about himself. Focus on his strengths. Let him know you trust that he will be able to find something else. Appreciate his efforts to provide for the family and show him you are confident in his ability to continue to do this.

APPRECIATE THAT HE PROTECTS (YOU AND THE FAMILY)

Whether your man is the main bread winner or not it is likely he will still pride himself on his ability to protect and look after the family.

The traditional way in which a man did this has changed, but he is still doing this and as I mentioned earlier, Steve has observed the way a man does this often goes unnoticed.

What you put your attention on is what the brain finds evidence of. I challenge you to look for evidence of your man doing little things with you and the family and then appreciate him for it.

Look for how he:

- Fixes things to keep you or your children safe or so you can enjoy something more.
- Pre-empts a dangerous situation and stops it from happening or steps up to 'save' you from a dangerous or scary situation (e.g. gets rid of spiders in the house).
- Takes over something so you don't get hurt or don't take on more than he thinks you can handle, like something heavy.
- Does things that he thinks will make you and the kids happier or make life better.

- Defends you or goes into bat for you either verbally or physically or talks about how he would do that.

Also take notice of the times you put him in that role and expect him to be the leader of the family in this way. Acknowledge your trust and confidence in him to protect and guide you in these situations.

Many of us have been indoctrinated to believe respect needs to be earned, but we don't realise often it may have already been earned, but we were too busy looking for evidence of what we were missing out on to notice.

To give a man respect, especially when you feel he has become disengaged or neglectful of you and the family, will require you to look harder at what his intentions are.

Even in a situation where your relationship is at breaking point, you can still find evidence of things you can respect him for.

This was something I pointed out to a friend of mine recently as she was moving out after her marriage break up. She had lost all confidence in her ex-partner being able to do anything for her and from what I could see, he had made it easy for her to come to these conclusions.

As she was going through the process of organising the move, she was trying to get him to help her and continually feeling frustrated by his efforts to help (or lack thereof).

I said to her *"it's never going to be the way you want it to be, however you've got to take what you are getting and appreciate that. He is helping. It may not be as much as you would like, but look at what he is doing, rather than what he isn't. He's helping in the way he knows how to."*

And he was helping her in little ways. He gave her money towards a new fridge. He hired a trailer, went and got the fridge and delivered it to her house, and after mucking her about on the second day of moving, he finally helped her to move some heavy things in the trailer.

I was at her new house unpacking her kitchen when he arrived with a trailer load of things. I could see he was really making an effort and was actually being quite helpful. He was asking her where she wanted things, helping her to move furniture, giving her suggestions on how to make it all more functional, and generally going above and beyond what we had expected.

When he left to get another load I challenged my friend to try a little experiment. I suggested to her that rather than notice what he wasn't doing, to genuinely appreciate what he was doing and sincerely thank him.

My friend had two dogs but the yard had no fence which would have been quite a mission for my friend to build. My experiment was to see if we could get him to build the fence willingly by her treating him with more respect.

I told her to only appreciate what she genuinely did appreciate and not to try and fake it or be over the top, but just to acknowledge what he was doing for her. At the very least just doing that would've made the interactions with each other a lot more amicable.

Then I suggested after she had done that to let it go for a couple of days and then casually ask for his advice about how to go about building the fence.

My experiment was to address what I'd learnt about how a man wants respect and see if that made a difference to his efforts to want to help her. Men like to be acknowledged for looking after their partners (even though she was now officially his ex), have their work ethic appreciated and for them to be acknowledged for their expertise and ability to problem solve.

It's important to note that for weeks before the move he had been very unco-operative and quite vindictive at times. I had already casually mentioned to him that he could perhaps build the fence and he gave me an emphatic, NO! We thought, if this experiment worked, then this story was going in this book because if this test worked on him, it could work on anyone!

I wasn't holding much hope that it would work, but just two days later my friend rang me to say the fence had been built.

Apparently after he had finished dropping the furniture at her house with a friend of his, she sincerely thanked him and told him it was very kind of him to have helped her out. She said he seemed to be hanging around and not looking to go anywhere.

They had a couple of drinks out the back and she said he was talking casually to her more than he had in months. The conversation ventured to the fence and she said, "*Well, I was going to ask you about that. I thought I might be able to get some suggestions from you as to what the best way to build it would be?*"

They chatted about it a bit more and then his friend winked at my friend and jumped on the band wagon. He said, "*Hmm, perhaps you'll have the dogs for longer because she won't be able to do all that on her own. She'll need someone to help her.*"

God love him for unknowingly catering to his friend's manly desires!

My friend's ex-partner responded well and said he would come back the next day and measure it up and give her his suggestions, still not saying that he would do it. She thanked him for his kindness and told him she really appreciated him doing that.

The next day he called her to say the fence had been built and that she owed him $60.

Now this experiment was not an attempt to manipulate him into doing something he didn't want to do. He had a choice not to do it.

Furthermore, it is likely he may have done it anyway without our experiment. However, if she had stayed annoyed with him and kept disrespecting him by speaking rudely to him there's no way he would've wanted to do anything for her.

Whether he would've built the fence or not will always be a mystery, but her showing him respect and appreciating his help definitely added to his willingness to do the job.

Also, it has now given my friend a new reference point for going into their new relationship as parents of their son. She will now experientially understand that the more she uses this understanding of men, the more she will get what she wants in return.

I share this story with you to help you to learn the same. You just cannot get more of what you want by depriving your partner of what they want!

Appreciate his desire to be the leader and to be in a position of authority.

"No man is going tell me what to do!" - That is what I grew up thinking. My mother watched her mother be submissive to her dad and subsequently became submissive to her husband for 20 years before she finally left.

Her leaving sent a very strong message to me as a girl heading into womanhood and because of what she experienced, my mother became a fiercely independent woman who knew how to look after and assert herself. She then had a completely opposite relationship where her new partner was the submissive one!

Needless to say, observing these roles as a child I grew up with an attitude towards my partners whenever I judged them to be trying to hold authority over me. My attitude was what originally turned Steve off me when he first met me, which I spoke about in my introduction.

> **The word 'authority' when used in a relationship context can cause many women to immediately get their back up. We have incorrectly substituted the word authority for domination and we fear giving our men any authority may lead us back into being submissive and powerless.**

Women have taken their power back, and rightly so, but now it's possible we've taken it to the other extreme and are oversensitive to any of our man's attempts at being assertive in the home.

I'm by no means saying a male has to have the end say in all matters, but it will mean a lot to him if he feels he has the end say in *some* matters and knows you respect his guidance.

I think one of the most confusing things for the modern man is to know when to take charge and when not to. Often women put him in a position of power or expect him to take charge, only to take it away from him or reprimand him if she believes he's done it wrong.

An example of this can be in the raising of his children. We may want him to step up and engage in the raising of his children, but if he does it wrong in our eyes we may undermine him in front of the children or criticise his efforts.

Another example: women are often the decision makers and have often become the leaders, but we often become tired and resentful of this role, not realising we have contributed to it being this way. We then complain to our partners that they're not doing enough or stepping up the way they should.

You may encourage him (or demand him) to take more initiative to do more for the family by handing over some of your responsibility.

You may tell him to help out more with the kids, do more around the house or take over the finances to reduce your workload.

You may send him the message that you want him to take more of an authoritative role in the family unit, but when he does you don't think it was good enough.

Perhaps he tried to become more engaging with the kids or in family matters but was shut down, lectured or you kept presenting him with a better way to do things and he gave up trying.

Remember a male thrives on being needed, but today's woman is often sending him a message that he's not needed, he's incompetent or he's not good enough to make her happy.

He wants to make you happy. He wants to feel needed. He innately needs to feel like he is fixing, helping and doing things to look after his family, but if he can't play this role and he doesn't know how to fix things, this is when he retreats. He'll do other things that do make him feel better, like work more or pursue other activities.

If you are a woman who wants her partner to step up then you need to trust him more and give him back some of the authority that he thrives upon.

This can be difficult for a woman to comprehend because we have been taught to resist being submissive to our husbands in any way. We've not learnt how to rely on our partner and how to communicate to him when it is okay to be in authority or how to be in authority in a respectful way.

We've not yet learnt how to balance the word submissive with reliance. This has left both sexes at odds - she feels resentful that he's not doing enough and he feels like he can never make her happy.

A client I had been working with had a wife who would criticise almost every move he made when he tried to help with family matters. One day their son had an orientation at school that she had to go to.

Knowing his wife would get stressed with the evening dinner, bath and bed routine with their other children, amongst getting reading for the orientation, he suggested she and his son leave the house early and make the occasion really special between her and her son.

He wanted to make her happy (as men ultimately do) and he would sort out the other kids with dinner and take care of everything.

Now, in her defence, this was a relatively new gesture for him to make. She had spent almost 10 years being the primary carer for the children and he had not been taking on a helpful role, at least not to this thoughtful degree.

She accepted his offer but gave him instructions that he make the other kids a healthy dinner - he needed to cook a meal from scratch.

Knowing what she was like and not wanting to upset her, he began listing all the potential things he could make for dinner and discussed what the 'right thing' to cook was.

My client didn't have a problem with this because he had realised that this was just one of those things that was important to her and he wanted to make her happy and prove to her he was changing and helping her.

This would have been the perfect opportunity to practice giving respect to her husband by giving him the authority to do what he needed to do to feed the kids and handle the evening routine. She could have appreciated what he was doing for her and trusted that his intentions were to do the best for his children that he could.

Imagine how empowering it would've been for him if she had said, *"Thank you honey for thinking of me. I really appreciate you doing that. Whatever you feed the kids will be fine. I know you can handle it."*

Chances are he would've been so chuffed at the respect and appreciation she gave him he probably would've wanted to do a stellar job and made them a great dinner in order to please her further because he knew she valued feeding her children healthy foods.

As women, our challenge is to let go of our defensiveness and our fear of being walked all over like our mothers were, or how their mothers were and to find a happy medium. We need to learn how to rely on our men more and they need to feel like we want to rely on them.

If he feels needed he will *want* to do more for you, which will make you feel more loved.

We need to learn that both sexes have strengths and weaknesses and to work *with* them. Both sexes can be the authority in unique ways in different situations and in other situations it can be an equal arrangement. We don't always have to lead, and nor do they.

It's important for women to remember that men need to feel needed. They don't want to be controlled or micromanaged any more than we do. If you trusted him more and had confidence in his abilities to take care of things, he would be more likely to step up to the plate.

However, at the same time we need to let go of our judgements and expectations that he will do it our way. He will do it his way and we need to be happy with that. We need to give him confidence that he will figure out how to do things if they are new to him, just like we had to. For example, finding ways of dealing with the children and their challenging behaviour. He's not stupid. It will make him feel good to figure it out because he's a fixer.

Trust that if he doesn't know how to do something, he will ask. Provide that safe space to let him do things for you, even if he's not great at it and let him know he can get your help if he needs it.

To make our men feel good about themselves we need to say things like, *"You'll be okay because you're a great dad. If you get stuck you can always ask me."* We need to trust our men have good intentions and want to keep us safe and to look after us.

For example, I have two sons and I have my female way of dealing with our boys' behaviour and Steve has his male way of dealing with them. As our boys left the toddler years and entered their young boy years it had become a bone of contention how to deal with certain behaviours in our sons. I felt he was too hard on them at times and Steve felt I was too soft.

One day Steve said to me, *"You don't know what it's like to be a boy. I have been a boy and I know how tough it can be growing up. Boys can be cruel and we need to teach our boys how to handle that. Sometimes the way you do it won't work for a boy."*

It was at that point I realised he was right. My boys were getting older and my loving and nurturing approach wasn't going to be what they always needed. They would always need my soft, loving motherly gestures, but what they also needed was a male's guidance.

I needed to trust in Steve's ability to know his own sex and be confident he knew what our boys needed. As a woman I simply did not have that insider knowledge.

I learnt I needed to step back and allow Steve to guide me and be the authority on the matter of raising our boys. It didn't mean I didn't ever disagree with him or I had no say in how we raised them. He didn't completely dominate all decisions, but I respected his expertise on the matter and I valued his opinion on how to best deal with their behaviour.

Although our decisions on how to raise the boys are still very much a joint effort, I have learnt that when Steve takes that tougher approach with our boys than I would I need to step back and trust his intentions are to help them to become strong, confident men.

If you want more love, then you need to let your partner lead more and allow him to make decisions - decide what is best for the family at times.

Trust, having confidence in his ability to protect his family, and the confidence he can figure things out and make the right decisions will be things you need to give him for him to feel more respected and thus feel more loving towards you.

Knowing when is the right time for you to have authority and for him to have authority or when it should be a joint approach will up to you as a couple, for everyone is different. This is a challenge of the modern day couple because those lines are very blurred compared with the old days.

As we continue on in Section C you will be guided more on how you can contemplate what works for you and your partner and how this division of authority can reach an equilibrium that both of you are happy with.

But he lets me have authority! I have to take charge or nothing would get done.

It is often the case that the man has given up trying to be an authority in the home. Either before he met you he learnt this is not the role he should play, or perhaps you have taught him through criticism and judgement that his way is not good enough and he's stopped trying.

Something to consider might be that this could be the reason he's not giving you the love you want. Perhaps that's why he may be coming across as being miserable.

In some cases, your partner may be depressed due to other areas of his life he feels he is not meeting perceived expectations. Perhaps for reasons that have nothing to do with you and the way you treat him he is feeling powerless and has taken on this powerless role in the home as well, believing he's not good enough.

Either way, giving him more authority without him fearing failure or judgement from you will likely cause a big shift in how he feels about himself and thus what he does around the home. You can give your man more authority by implementing some of the following:

- Let him make more decisions and don't challenge him on them.
- Say "how would you like us to do this?" or "let's do it your way".
- Ask for his opinions and suggestions and then follow them.
- Thank him for taking charge of something.
- Trust him to do things when he's taking charge and have confidence that his intention is to protect and look after his family.
- Don't criticise him for mistakes he makes when he does take charge because no one is perfect. Be okay that he won't always make the right decisions, just like you don't.
- Resist the urge to tell him what to do or undermine his decisions with criticism.
- Realise you aren't always right and your way isn't the only way to do something.
- Instead of criticising the way he's done something when he takes initiative, say nothing or give appreciation that he attempted it.
- When you disagree with his decisions, start by appreciating his standpoint on the matter and ask to express your standpoint to create an alignment.

When it comes to authority in the home someone has to take the lead. In a modern day world that someone is not always male and isn't always female. To have an equal relationship means sometimes the man is going to take charge and sometimes the woman will. It won't always be both.

It will be up to both of you as a couple to distinguish those lines when it comes to the important things and to allow give and take to occur over the little things.

As a woman be conscious of your indoctrinated tendencies to take over, micro-manage and criticise his desire to be in authority with you or the kids and learn how to back off, say nothing and let him do it his way sometimes.

Recognise in yourself an attitude of trying to assert yourself when he's trying to be in charge and recognise any fears of vulnerability you have when relying on your partner to take charge.

The key is not to see this as being walked all over, but as being willing to compromise and acknowledge how good it makes him feel to be able to be the leader he innately wants to be.

He wants to guide his family in a direction that he feels is right, just like you do. Allowing him to do this will work wonders for his self-esteem, not to mention what it will do to improve his treatment of you.

APPRECIATE HIS DESIRE TO FIX PROBLEMS AND BE THE EXPERT

This one goes hand in hand with the previous desire to want to be in authority. Men pride themselves on being an expert.

Historical male roles have set our men up to be this way because they were the ones that had the worldly knowledge. Women were the experts in homecare and child raising but other knowledge about life was largely learnt from men.

It's only in today's world that women have become just as knowledgeable as men.

However, this doesn't mean men don't still like to feel acknowledged for what they know. We all do to a degree. However for men this is something they feel particularly chuffed about.

Men are fixers. It's what they innately do. They tinker with and build things – their motorbikes, cars, computers or other mechanical or technological things. They fix problems on TV, like footy or politics. They are generally the experts when it comes to outdoor activities like camping, fishing or sports.

When it comes to these things, women are often happy to let go of the reins, but we can also tend to want to take over and tell our men what to do. This makes them feel disrespected. It makes them feel like we don't trust them to be able to do it.

Since I have begun to understand what makes the majority of men tick I have become self-aware of just how often I add my two cents worth in when it's really not necessary.

I have told Steve how to drive, where to park and what direction to go when heading out. I've told him what to cook, how to cook and how to do the dishes.

I have found myself offering him 'unsolicited advice' left, right and centre and have had to make a considerable effort to stop myself from doing that. I didn't realise how often I did this until now.

If you are a 'need to be right' woman (like I am known to be) then this tip is the one that will earn you the most brownie points and also the one that will take the most effort to curb.

This tip is really about being able to let your partner be the expert and recognise his desire to want to help you and fix things for you.

Telling him what to do and giving him 'unsolicited advice' makes him frustrated because he wants to feel like he is doing it. He doesn't want to be told what to do.

Rather than say, "Can you do this?" Say, "would it be okay if you do this?" I have found if I ask Steve to do something in a way that makes him feel like he has an option to help or not, he will more likely help me without getting cranky. Also, if he is helping around the house, I have learnt not to tell him how I would like him to help or what to do next, as this can get on his nerves too.

Let him help in his way. You might find he begins to help and then ends up fixing something else. He's still doing something to help you, it's just not in the way you would like it to be. Recognise what he is doing rather than what he isn't doing.

If you are experiencing a problem ask your partner what he would do. Allow him to make suggestions.

If you are doing something he is an expert on, ask for his opinion or his suggestions on how to do it better. Chances are he might even do it for you or have some really good ideas on how you can do it.

You will show him the ultimate respect if you value his suggestions and opinions on how to fix a problem rather than dictating your solution. He will feel needed if he can provide a solution that will make you happier and feel like he's done his job as a partner.

Men are traditionally very practical and good at solving problems. It's often very clear to them 'what to do'. Let him show you this and don't give the impression you don't need his help.

But I don't want him to 'fix' me

One of the most frustrating things to a woman can be when she is talking about a problem and he is trying to offer solutions. He can come across as being dismissive, self-righteous or very black and white. This is because he is trying to make you happy by fixing your problems or because it's just plain habit that he goes into 'fix it' mode.

Next time he does this, rather than get upset at him, recognise his good intentions and remember he doesn't know that you are talking to feel better. He doesn't know he just needs to listen.

You could try telling him directly, *"Thank you for trying to help me with this. I appreciate it. I think what I need right now is your help in just hearing me talk it out. I'm just venting right now and don't really need a solution."*

If he struggles to understand that (because it is such a foreign concept to a man) perhaps ring a girlfriend instead.

Appreciate his need for time, space & activity

A woman's worth is heavily reliant upon the quality of her relationships. She values connection, support, nurturing, love and companionship.

When a male withdraws she can feel rejected or hurt, incorrectly feeling like he is dismissing her or that he doesn't love her as much.

"Why does he need to go out with the boys?"

"Why does he seem like he's going off sulking whenever there's a problem?"

"Why does he spend hours working on that stupid car and won't spend any time with me?"

"Why can't he be happy just being at home with me and the kids? Why does he have to plan time away? Doesn't he love me?"

When men make plans away from the family it can be confusing for a woman. She can often see it as a sign of rejection or evidence he doesn't love her.

However, what's really going on is something different.

Women connect by talking and giving and receiving support from another person.

Men connect through experiences. They need to engage in activities and things they are interested in. Often they don't find what women do interesting and that has nothing to do with whether he loves you or not.

A man prides himself on achievement. There's not really any achievement in sitting around talking. He wants to do things, fix things, make things or engage in activities with a purpose.

His need for time away from his partner & the family

On a primal level a man can still be the hunter he used to be. In the modern day of huge financial responsibilities and the pressure of doing more around the home and being more engaged with the family a man can feel like a caged animal, chomping at the bit for some freedom to be that primal man free of all the rules of society (and the rules from his partner).

Men need to *'run with wolves'*. They need to be with other men. They need to connect with their primal roots. They need the freedom to be loud, swear, fart, be disgusting, drink, shoot the breeze, be carefree, and to take a break from responsibilities. Sometimes he'll like doing this with the family. Other times he will need to do it on his own or with his friends, depending on his character.

It doesn't mean he doesn't love his partner. In fact he'll love her more if she can understand this need and be cool with him taking a break from his world.

When women take a break from their responsibilities they might go to dinner with friends to talk more or engage in activities to connect with friends. Her weekends away usually involve spa retreats, relaxing by a pool, being pampered and nurtured or just hanging out with a girlfriend for coffees and chats.

Women often won't allow themselves to take a break because they either feel they are neglecting their responsibilities as a mum or they don't trust their partner to be able to look after their children. She can be her own worst enemy and not know how to rely on her partner or ask for his help. She often won't let herself take time out and thus becomes resentful of him taking time out either.

She may complain she doesn't get to do the things he does, but the problem is that she doesn't make it a priority, whereas he does. He may recognise that he needs to take a break and so he does, whereas she may not.

Perhaps she does take time out, but not as much as he does because she doesn't feel it is necessary. She may not understand why he has to do the things he does or go to the extremes he does when he gets that break. She might be happy with a short break to catch up with her friends, whereas he may need more.

Men just aren't wired like women and it's important that women respect they are different. He feels good about himself by doing things.

- Playing video games makes him feeling like he's succeeding, so it makes him feel good. It relaxes him to escape from life.
- Going out into his shed and playing with his car or motorbike or building something makes him feel like he's achieving something.
- Going camping or fishing relaxes him and gives him the freedom to get back to his grass roots, to get primal, to be dirty and not have to shower and be impressive or attentive to his partner.
- Going to the footy and drinking with the boys helps him to unwind, have fun and be himself away from the pressures of work and looking after his wife and children's needs.

Sometimes men just need the space to do things by themselves or with other blokes who understand the rules of being a bloke. Men don't give men unsolicited advice. They don't try to control each other, micro-manage their moves, tell them their decisions are wrong, try to change them or tell each other what to do. Men don't tell each other that they need to act a certain way, drink less, be quiet, stop farting, stop being disgusting, talk more, or be responsible. They too want to engage in activity and achieve, fix and escape from their worlds. They get each other, just like women understand each other. That's why both sexes need friendships.

If you can respect his friendships and acknowledge his need to spend time alone doing whatever he needs to, or engaging in activities with friends without feeling guilty, you will probably find he will want to spend more time with you.

Of course some men take this to an extreme or take you for granted, so this is where you both need to be open about discussing what works for both of you.

Make sure you are getting time out as well and it's not always about him. Don't get caught up in keeping tabs on who is spending more time away from the family. Remember both of you are wired differently. A female might be content with just a couple of hours catching up with a friend, whereas he may need a whole day or a weekend away.

Perhaps you are okay with a weekend of pampering while he plans a whole week boy's trip away once or twice a year.

It's also important to assess whether you might already feel like you are getting adequate time out and don't understand why he needs to be away from the family when you don't. Often as women who are stay-at-home mums or part-time workers we get more opportunities to connect with our friends.

We may meet up at play groups or school events and get our social fixes that way, thus not really feeling a need to literally socialise away from the family. That is why it's not about negotiating equal time out but more focussing on what each other feels they need.

Parenting is a tough job and both mums and dads need their space to enjoy individual activities away from their children (and often their spouses).

Let your partner know you respect that he needs his time out but you also expect that it will need to be planned and agreed upon so that it works for the family. At least, most of the time anyway.

If he's going to have a night out with the boys it can't always be a spur of the moment thing if you have something else planned the next day because that's not fair on you.

Similarly though, if you know he's having a night out with the boys don't plan anything for the next day where you need him involved and then get annoyed that he's a lump on the couch that can't move because he's too hung over. Don't make him suffer the next day because of his sickness, just because drinking to that degree is not an activity you wouldn't engage in because that's not fair on him.

Be cool with him to unwind in his way and again trust that he wants to be the provider and protector of the family. Most men have good intentions but often aren't given the credit to show their intentions.

JUST BE THERE

Sometimes when he's out in the shed or working on something at home, he may even like it if you were to join him and just be there with him. Get interested in what he's doing or just sit there and read a book and that can make him feel connected to you.

Try it out. I'll often hear Steve say, *"come and talk to me while I do this."*

Did you ever do this when you first met and didn't have children? You may have watched him work, sat with him while he fished or just went for a drive with him? He may like it when you do this, providing you aren't telling him what to do, nagging him or criticising him.

Men pride themselves on doing things. It's just how they're wired. Sometimes going to the movies, going out to dinner and just being with you cuddling on a couch isn't interesting to him. It's got nothing to do with him not loving you.

I think this tip is one where you have to recognise the needs of men are very different to the needs of women when it comes to time out. By understanding this tip and giving your partner his space guilt free, you will find he is much more responsive to your needs.

A GENERAL NEED FOR SPACE

You may argue that he already is taking more time out – much more than you would like. However I would ask you to consider whether he is getting the respect in other areas as well? Do you criticise him when he is home? Do you make him feel guilty for taking that time out? Does he feel liked and needed when he is around at home? Does he feel acknowledged for the work he does and how much he does for the family?

When women have a problem or are involved in an argument they want to talk it out. Often men want to retreat. They need time to think about the problem and come up with a solution. Sometimes men have a testosterone build up to contend with and need some time to calm down. He will do this by walking away from an argument or engaging in another activity.

Sometimes he needs to unwind from his day with some time for himself. However, a woman can see this as being irresponsible or uncaring, or she can feel rejected when he does this. She may even feel unsupported, especially if she has been with the children all day while he's been at work and then he comes home and engages in an activity that isn't helpful to her.

Don't be offended if he retreats to his cave after work or when having an argument. Instead recognise where it is coming from and negotiate how you can get what you want, while he gets what he wants.

It may be important to establish a wind down time for him where perhaps he goes somewhere before coming home for a half hour or so to unwind and then comes home ready for helping out.

Often when women share their feelings they do so by airing them with criticism. A classic mistake women make is highlighting their partner's flaws in the hope it will wake their partners up and encourage them to be more loving. However it's actually having the opposite effect.

If you can acknowledge his need to calm down, walk away or unwind by having space and negotiate a better way he can do that which will also work for you too, it will be a much easier conversation to have.

For example, *"I understand when you finish work you need some time to unwind, but that time of the day is tough for me too. What do you think we can do to work together on this so you can come home ready to help? Is there somewhere you can go first to unwind and then come home?"*

Another example might be to say, *"When things get heated, can you just tell me you need some space to think or that you need some time out and then I'll know what's happening for you and we can work out a plan for you to do this, because I realise this is important for you."*

SOME MEN DON'T HAVE FRIENDS

There are some men who don't really have friends or don't really feel the need to do things that traditionally men do, however their desire for time out may present itself in other ways.

Perhaps he just enjoys reading a book or doing something a bit quieter. Perhaps he might prefer to play computer games.

It's important to discuss with him what he wants and not to assume he needs time out like other men do. It's not wrong for him to be this way.

In this case it is important to understand his desire to stay at home, rather than engage in other activities. Perhaps you'll find what he does for his time out is by himself doing something, building something or fixing something. Perhaps you may find there is something else going on for him that explains why he doesn't have male friendships.

A friend of mine's partner didn't have any good male friends. They had friends they did social family activities with, but he wasn't good enough friends with the males to spend time one on one. On one side of things he didn't feel an urgent need to have friends, but on the other side of things he just wasn't interested in doing the things that most men he knew wanted to do. He didn't drink, wasn't really interested in the footy and wasn't a loud and primal man. He didn't really want *to 'run with wolves'*.

So it wasn't that he didn't want friends. It was more that he didn't know how to make friends that shared his interests or where to find them.

So his family was where he got most of his pleasure. The problem there was that he couldn't understand his wife's need for social engagement outside of the family. He didn't understand why she wanted to go out drinking with her friends when he wanted to stay at home.

In this case, it's important you highlight that you are both different when it comes to time out and it's not a reflection of your commitment to your family, just something you enjoy doing. Just as with a male going out and doing his activities, it's equally important for a woman to be considerate of the family unit and to plan her time out and negotiate the boundaries with her partner so it works for everyone.

Sometimes a man also has some guilt over taking time out, feeling like he is neglecting his family by doing so. Again, your encouragement and reassurance will be helpful here so he knows it's okay by you and you respect his need to do so.

Time out is a big issue between men and women and I realise in many cases the man is often living in the past and not taking on the responsibilities of being a family man.

If this is occurring then a woman needs to reflect on two things:

a) Has she somehow contributed to the set-up of this dynamic? Has she taken over doing everything such as the previous examples of how you can easily teach people how to treat you?

OR

b) Does he really need this time out and you are thinking he should be home more often? Are you neglecting to respect his need for time out, or is he not feeling respected when he is home and thus feels more drawn to escaping his responsibilities?

I realise one person changing things in a relationship doesn't repair a relationship. It takes two to make it and it takes two to break it. However, often it can only take one of you to get the ball rolling.

When it comes to time out you can be very influential by understanding his need for respect in all areas, including his need for space, and you will likely see a very different reaction to how he is towards you. When you stop the 'I hurt you because you hurt me' game the walls come down and alignment can then be discussed.

Remember, someone has to be the hero of the relationship and perhaps this is one way you can do it – by allowing him his much needed space without getting offended and without making him feel guilty.

You just also have to make sure your needs are also being adequately met too so there is no resentment.

APPRECIATE HIS NEED FOR SEXUALITY

Men need sex. I'm sorry ladies but this is not a choice for him. It is a physical need. I know you are over hearing this, but this is a fact.

For men a sexual act eases the testosterone pressure he constantly feels and it will actually soften him to be more of the man you want him to be.

Often when men bring up the issue of sex, women get defensive. They retort that it shouldn't matter how much he gets it. That if he loved her he wouldn't be with her just for the sex.

She may get offended if he looks at other women and see it as a sign he doesn't think she's attractive.

When women criticise and make men wrong, they shut down and they stop talking. However, I encourage you to ask your man more about what it's like to want sex more often. Ask him why he feels the need to have it and really get a clear understanding of why it's so important to him.

Whether lack of sex is a running joke in your relationship or a serious issue, it is often a bone of contention between couples. I am convinced it is because of a gross misunderstanding about how men think about sex and why it is such a burning desire for them.

Sex is often an issue with couples because of the similar cycle we've been talking about with relationships in general.

Women are saying, you give me more love, romance and affection and

I'll give you more sex.

Men might say, you give me more sex and I'll give you more love, romance and affection.

Women withhold sex until they get more love and affection just like they withhold respect until they get more love.

Men withhold love until they get more sex, but what us women don't realise is that doing this may not really be a choice.

This article from the Huffington post, although romanticising it, explains it quite well:

<u>Men and Sex – The Real Truth</u>
by Doug and Leslie Gustafson
cited from Huffington Post article, 19th August, 2013[1]

For many men, sexual contact opens up a gateway to their soul. Like turning on a spigot of running water, they suddenly get in touch with raw feelings, the virtues of tenderness and the need to depend on another human being for warmth and safety. Men become softer and more human in that they gain access to a wider variety of feelings, thoughts and emotions. Moving, consistent sex turns their world upside down. Their heart inside out. Their love for life and wife bubble up from a deep well of feelings they often wall off, becoming clearer like a camera lens bringing its target into focus.

Most men have no history of positive role models for how to treat women, what real intimacy looks like and how to translate their needs for closeness into a positive way of pursuing their lover. And this is the rub! Think about it.

Women want men who open up their feminine heart and body skilfully. Like a finely wrapped gift, they don't want the beautiful

---

1. http://www.huffingtonpost.com/doug-and-leslie-gustafson/men-and-sex-the-real-trut_b_3781240.html

wrapping paper and ribbon hurriedly ripped off, wadded up and tossed into the garbage. They want to experience profound safety, honour and excitement in how men approach them, hold them and ask to be inside. Men, on the other hand, are quite capable of "paving the way" to intimacy -- after the fact. They surrender to their feminine, touchy-feely side during and after sex. During and after!

What a chasm in timing. Men want sex, which helps move them into a deeper connection with all their emotional wants and needs. Women want that deeper connection before the bedroom door opens. Ultimately, they both want the same thing. Passionate, rock-the-bed-stand, earthquake sex with souls bared wide open in tenderness, connection and erotic touch. And orgasms that spell not only physical release, but the intersection of two souls who need a deep kind of love suspended in time, delivered with expertise and boat-floating sexiness.

As author Eggerichs says in his book Love and Respect: *"The rule that never changes is: you can't get what you need by depriving your partner of what your partner needs."*

This also applies to sex too.

Women connect through talking and drawing their partner closer to them. They already know how to share their feelings and love other people.

This doesn't always come as easy to men. Men need sex as a way to soften, connect and open up - just as women want them to.

However, bombarded with images of sex-mad, aggressive monsters or womanisers from TV, music videos, movies and magazines, men have been depicted as just wanting to 'have their way' with their women and release their needs with whoever will let them. Men have gotten a hard rap.

A lot of women don't realise that sex *is* their way of connecting. Good, intimate sex *will* open up those heartfelt channels she is looking for. It just may not seem like it because she has become so disinterested in it. Often sex has become that much of a chore that he has given up trying to please her and is doing it purely for his own release of tension whenever she feels obligated enough to give it to him.

I, myself, misunderstood Steve's desire for connection in this way until I did the research for this book. I always understood that men needed sex and I fulfilled my obligatory duties whether I wanted it or not, at least once a week because I knew it would make him feel better physically. I could see the testosterone build up coming out in his impatience when he didn't get that release.

I mistakenly thought by fulfilling my duties as a wife, even though I still enjoyed it, he would be satisfied. But often he would voice to me that he didn't like it when I wasn't into it.

It was fair to say his release still freed his testosterone build up, but I wasn't quite understanding the connection part. I hadn't realised that the times that I was really into it he became more affectionate and loving.

Now I get it and now I'm loving it!

Incidentally, now that I am getting more affection and love by being more into sex I seem to want more sex. It's ironic really.

When you appreciate his need for sex, not just as a release that makes him happier but on an emotional level, rather than seeing it as reflective of his insensitivity or him being selfish, sex becomes a whole different experience.

Women have forgotten or don't understand in the first place that a man wants to please her and connect with her. Just because he's big and strong doesn't mean he's exempt from hurt or needing love. Often sexual rejection for a man means personal rejection.

Everyone wants to love and be loved. Behind that person with an uncontrollable physical need for sex is still a person needing to be loved. As Steve Biddulph states in his book, *Manhood*, *"we men feel pretty lucky if our partner asks what we would like to do in bed. But the most magical woman is the one who asks what we would like to feel."*

Men and women often have a different love language. Understand that love language and you will have a completely different relationship. This is what I am attempting to teach you in this book.

Your man is not the enemy. He too wants what you want. I challenge you to try a little experiment. Give him as much sex as he wants for the next two weeks and work at being totally into it.

Think about pleasuring him and allowing him to pleasure you. Ask him what he wants to feel and be a little more adventurous than you normally are. Above all try to have fun with it.

See what happens when you do. You can always go back to the way it was before if it doesn't work.

However if it does work, you may find yourself experiencing a completely different relationship. Perhaps this might be the thing to break down those walls that have been put up between the two of you.

Furthermore, if you do this in conjunction with respecting (appreciating) his work ethic, his leadership and desire for authority, allow him to fix your problems and be the expert and give him some guilt free time out in his way, he won't know what's hit him.

You may find that he softens and treats you more lovingly. You may find he wants to do more for you and spend more time at home with you. You may find he offers to take you out or does random romantic things. You may find he opens up and starts to talk to you about the relationship and how to create alignment in your issues.

You may find yourself faced with a completely different relationship, moving closer to the one you want.

Yes, giving a man sex can be that powerful!

When you show a man more respect by appreciating these areas we have talked about in this chapter, you will see a shift in him. You will see him soften and open up. He will talk to you more and you will begin to be able to connect with him in the ways you've always wanted to.

Bring back your trust in him to love, protect and provide for you and allow him to be the leader he wants to be. Let go of your old reference points and give him a chance to be the man you want him to be. Allow him to step up to the plate in his own way and recognise the way he does it as being valuable.

Remember, what you put your attention on is what you'll find evidence of. Look for what you can appreciate about him and then tell him.

Sometimes it is difficult to respect because of the behaviour, but what you need to do is respect the human behind the behaviour. Respect that innate goodness is there and look for what he is doing that is worthy of respect instead of focussing on what he isn't doing.

Ask yourself: Is he responding in an unloving way because he is feeling disrespected? Will what I say or do next come across as being disrespectful or unappreciative of his efforts?

To finish this chapter, I'd like to leave you with a quote I found on a forum that sums up perfectly what most men want from their partners:

MY TIP FOR WIVES:

Love your man, give him free reign to do things he loves (e.g. don't make him think he needs your approval to do something that you know he really loves), expect him to act like a man and treat you as a woman, and ravage him at least every couple of weeks and you will never lose him. You will also gain a friend who would move the world for you. I just wished I had married such a *woman*.

Chapter Nine

FOR MEN:
WHAT WOMEN WANT & HOW TO GIVE THEM MORE LOVE

Women ultimately want connection, support and evidence she is loved, nurtured, understood and cared for. She is constantly looking for evidence that reassures her she is loved.

Write that out and stick it somewhere where you will absorb it and remember it. It is likely to be your key to getting more respect and, just quietly, possibly getting more sex. Women want more sex when they feel your relationship is intimate. Intimacy to her is connection and love.

There are four categories that will help you to understand how to show love to a woman.

- Communication and connection
- Understanding
- Saying 'I'm Sorry'
- Reassurance and acknowledgement

Master the art of figuring out what works best for your partner and you will find her responding to you in a completely different way.

Understanding & Support

Fire up those listening skills boys, because this is really important to a woman. As you know, she talks…a lot. But you have to know that she's doing it for a reason.

She's doing it because she needs to feel understood and supported.

You can do this by listening when she's talking. Shut off the TV (or get yourself Tivo or Foxtel IQ so you can pause your show) and actually hear what she's saying.

Make eye contact with her and really try and understand what she's saying. Ask her questions to find out more. Get interested in what she's saying. You don't even really have to answer her unless she's asking a question.

Some regular responses to show you are listening is all she needs. "*Yeah, right.*" "*Oh, I see.*" "*Hmmm.*" "*Yeah, I can see that.*" "*That must be tough.*" Anything that lets her know you're following what she's saying and you are listening is going to win you some serious brownie points.

Take notice of your body language. I was counselling a couple the other day and observed that when she was talking he had a completely vacant look on his face. His body language did not show any evidence that he was listening at all, let alone considering what she was saying. This wasn't the case, however because when I asked him what he'd heard her say he was able to articulate it back perfectly. Yet from an outsider point of view who wasn't emotionally attached, I could not see any evidence that he could have cared less about what she was saying, so imagine how she must be feeling and interpreting her response. Be mindful of your body language because it speaks volumes about your interest in her.

Look at today's role of a woman - she is busy and she's got a lot on her plate and thus a lot on her mind. A woman connects by sharing her innermost thoughts and feelings. If you dismiss that need in her, she feels you don't care about her and what's happening in her life.

She needs to know you understand what's happening for her and that you are supporting her 100 percent.

Sometimes what she's discussing with you might seem trivial and not even a problem and you may be tempted to be dismissive about it or not see it as an important discussion, however be mindful that her talking to you is not just about the issue, it's about the connection she's trying to get from you, particularly if she is feeling bad about something. She will be looking for love and support to feel better. You listening to her will give her that.

Avoid your tendency to want to fix the situation too. If she's not directly asking for an answer to her problem, then assume she is just venting and needing your support and understanding. If you're not sure, ask. *"Do you want me to help you with this or are you just talking things through?"*

You can show her your support by asking her to tell you how you can help more or give her what she needs.

If she's complaining about a problem and you really want to fix it, rather than present her with solutions that will only fire her up more, calm her down by encouraging her to show you how you can help. Chances are, if she's just venting, she will say something like, *"there's nothing you can really do."*

But inside, she's cheering that you've even bothered to ask. At the end of the conversation, she may even say, *"thank so much for listening. I really appreciate it."* There you go, there's some appreciation (i.e. respect) already.

COMMUNICATION & CONNECTION

By far this is the most important aspect of a woman you need to understand if you want things to change.

Women talk to connect. It's just what they do. It's a reality men will have to come to terms with if they want an amicable relationship.

Saying things like *'let's just drop it'* or saying *'I've had enough'* and walking off when you are facing conflict is really difficult for her to comprehend. It makes sense to you because males tend to want to go in their caves to figure it out for themselves or talk to exchange information or solve a problem they can't fix themselves.

However a women is talking to get close to you. She wants to resolve the conflict then and there to keep the connection.

WHY DOES SHE KEEP BRINGING UP THE PAST?

Because she's trying to tell you the issue hasn't been resolved for her. She literally can't let it go, or drop it because she doesn't feel as connected with you as she'd like if the issue remains unresolved. She wants to sort it out so she can feel closer to you.

WHY DOES SHE TRY TO CONTROL ME?

Often men find women ask too many questions. He can feel like she is trying to control him or interrogate him.

Women don't talk to control. They talk to connect. She's not trying to control you, she's trying to control how she is loved. Remember a lot of women don't know how to ask for love because they're still stuck in an old generational pattern of fighting for their rights. Perhaps she thinks demanding your love is the way to get it, not realising it is actually taking her further from the goal. This is where you will need to understand her ignorance and give her what she wants to soften her enough to give you what you need.

If she's going off her tree you can soften her by inviting her to talk about how she's feeling and showing an interest in wanting to understand her position. Remember Steve's approach to me walking out of an argument from my introduction? He said to me, "*Stop. Come here. Where are you going? Talk to me.*" In that moment, my whole demeanour changed. I already felt understood and I hadn't even said anything!

He introduced me to the concept of not fighting, but just talking more. Sometimes you need to be that for your partner because she has lost confidence there is any point in talking to you.

It can be this loss of confidence that can lead her into finding solace in her friends and forgetting to bother even trying to connect with you, or worse, she finds this need in another man who understands a woman's need to talk.

When she is asking lots of questions she is trying to bring you closer to her. She's trying to understand you, support you and connect with you because that's what she would want you to do for her.

If you feel like all this talking is way too much and you need to take a break from the conversation, do so by saying something like: *"I just need some time to think about what we've been talking about."* That way she feels like you regard the situation as important to you too.

Or you could say, *"I know you've had a rough day. I understand it's been full on for you. Do you mind if we keep talking about this later. I just need to go and have a shower and wind down from my day."* She may still feel a little dismissed, but nowhere near what she would if you dismissed her with, *"Oh do you ever stop whingeing. I've had enough."*

When she complains I feel like she's blaming me

When women criticize and complain and the man is somehow involved in her complaint, he may interpret that as meaning something critical about him – a direct attack on his character. He may retreat or fight back.

Men often get defensive and angry or withdraw. Stop. Listen. Hear her. Don't personalise what she's saying as meaning she's disrespecting you. Consider her perspective *in that moment*. How has she come to believe what she's saying? Is it a valid argument? Does she have genuine grounds for feeling the way she does? What is your contribution to the problem?

Don't take everything she says literally either. She often uses words like 'always', 'all the time' or 'never' to emphatically describe what she's feeling. She knows it's not all the time. She doesn't mean these things literally. It's just her way of showing you her level of conviction – how important this is to her.

What she's really telling you is that she is feeling your actions make her question how much you care about her and her feelings.

SHE'S NEVER HAPPY. SHE'S ALWAYS COMPLAINING.

Remember women have a tendency to want to talk about several problems at once. Even more of a reason not to try and fix, as you'll do your head in trying to keep up. Just talking about the problem will help her to make more sense of it. She will make herself feel better in a lot of cases and all you need to do is resonate with her and let her know her feelings are validated.

To a man, women seem to bring up silly little problems that don't mean much to a man. This is her way of keeping things connected with you and keeping the relationship healthy. When there's a problem, she wants to talk about it, air it out and clean it up before it gets any bigger. This can come across to a man as *'she's always whingeing at me'*. **She's not whingeing. She's connecting**.

Sometimes she'll bring up issues that just can't be resolved right now and that frustrates a man greatly because he wants to fix it too, but can't. He personalises it when she keeps bringing the subject up because he just wants to be able to fix it, but there just may not be a solution available right now.

She's doing this because she wants her relationships clean and up to date and she probably see's that subject as being detrimental to that goal. Her bringing that up over and over is not an attack on you, it's her also wanting to see the situation fixed, and thus her relationship too.

SIMPLE TIPS TO CONNECT WITH WOMEN

- A loving look, a touch as you walk past her or smiling at her.
- Asking if you can help with something.
- Talk to her about her day and tell her about yours.
- Give her a kiss and a hug hello when you see her after work or if she's been at work.

- Make regular eye contact when you are talking. Looking equals listening to her, so no watching the footy while she's talking about her day or her problems.
- Give her affection without the expectation of sex - huge brownie points for this one will often get you more action in bed in the long run.
- Make an effort to spend time together, alone. Go for a walk, take her to dinner, spend some time with the TV off after the kids are in bed.
- Organise spontaneous gestures that show her you care – a surprise outing you have organised, including getting a babysitter, or a surprise massage. Do something for her that she wouldn't expect you to do.
- Make a big deal of anniversaries and birthdays. They are an important way to provide reassurance to her. Men often value possessions, but a meaningful, thoughtful present that shows that you understand her likes and what would make her happy will go a long way. Women don't always need expensive gestures to feel loved.
- Remember what she has been doing or working on and ask her how it went. Help her to take a break. Sometimes women get so caught up in their world of perfection they forget to take a break. She will feel so supported and understood if you did something to make her take a break. I know when Steve stands up to me and says, *"Jack, stop it. Just sit down. I'll take care of it. You've been running around all day. You need to take a break,"* - my goodness that means the world to me.

One dad I worked with booked a weekend away and organised the babysitters. She whinged and complained she didn't have time and that things would be too unorganised if she took the time out, but he stood his ground and said those things would be there when they came back and that while they were away she would enjoy being away from them. I assured him it would be good for her to realise that the world wouldn't end if she wasn't there for one weekend and she would appreciate the gesture.

However, a word of warning in regards to this last one. When she's in problem sharing mode, she is venting to feel better about herself and is looking to be heard and understood. If you try this tip while she's doing this, it is possible she will feel dismissed and perceive you as being insensitive and uncaring.

REASSURANCE & ACKNOWLEDGEMENT

Deliberately take time to appreciate what she does for you. Women often say they want respect as well - it's not just men who need more respect in a relationship. However, why they need respect is different than why a man wants respect.

> **A man wants respect as confirmation he is good enough. A woman wants respect because it shows her you understand her stresses and you care that she has a heavy work load. Acknowledgment for a woman shows her you love her.**

Showing your appreciation for what she does for you and the family will give her the reassurance that she's **doing a good job.**

Look at the role of a woman today and the internal tug of war we talked about earlier. Whether she is a stay at home mum wrestling with fears around being good enough as 'just a mum', or whether she is a working mum wrestling with fears that she's not being 'a good enough mum', or just feeling like she's often questioning herself anyway, your reassurance of her abilities will go a long way.

I struggled big time when my children were little. Anxiety, depression, unhappiness, whingeing, complaining - the works. I had it all going on. One of the things I remember Steve saying over and over again was: "I *couldn't do what you do. I couldn't stay at home with the kids and deal with what you deal with."*

Do you know how much those two really simple sentences meant to me at the time? It told me that it wasn't just me finding it difficult. I didn't feel alone in my anguish. I felt understood.

Women are looking for their partner's reassurance. The modern day woman is questioning her appearance, her abilities, how she parents, how she balances all of her needs with everyone else's, whether she's doing a good enough job, and whether she's doing it as well as other women. The list goes on.

Wherever you can reassure her that she is doing a good job, that you are proud of her, that you acknowledge how hard she has it, or how difficult it must be for her, she will feel enormous gratitude. She will feel supported and she will feel understood.

You are likely to get more appreciation and respect for it in return too.

SAYING "I'M SORRY"

This might be a difficult one to some men because it can feel like you are compromising dignity and respect, or giving away your power.

However, try to change your perspective on it. Rather than looking at what you think you'll lose look at what you're likely to gain. You won't lose your respect. Rather you will gain respect because she is feeling understood and connected with you.

She will appreciate (respect) you for 'being man enough' to say it.

That said, I do not mean just saying sorry for any little thing she thinks you are doing wrong.

Admit when you are *genuinely* wrong. Saying sorry, for me, was difficult in the early stages of my own relationships. Steve must've had a dad who really 'got it' to teach him how to handle a woman, because he taught me how to say I'm sorry.

When I would discuss a problem, he would often genuinely listen to what I was saying and think about my perspective. When he understood my side of things, he would often say, *"I can see how you would think that. Sorry, babe, I didn't mean to make you feel that way."* Or he would say, *"I get that. I'm sorry you felt that way but that wasn't my intention. I just meant….."* and then he would voice his perspective.

"I get that" and "I can see how you would think that" implied his understanding.

The "I'm sorry" would show me he cared about my feelings and wanted to resolve the issue.

Those two simple little worlds help women to resolve an issue and move on from it. They are so important to her feeling like she has resolved conflict and reconnected with you. You may just have to swallow your pride and let her hear them – providing of course you feel they are warranted.

As a child there were some difficult times with my Dad. When I was about 18 years old I went to lunch with my Dad and our conversation gravitated to my childhood. I was able to tell him how I felt about my childhood and the repercussions of my experiences with him on my self-esteem. He listened like I'd never had him listen before and at the end of our lunch we were driving home when out of the blue he said, *"I'm really sorry I made you feel that way."*

Right then and there I was able to let go of everything I'd ever held onto about my childhood.

You've know idea how powerful those words are to a woman. Saying sorry for a woman is just as good as saying I love you and totally understand you - providing it is said with conviction

She wants to be understood and **she wants to hear you say sorry.** This is really important as it shows her you have taken the time to consider your part in the problem and are making an effort to improve the situation and work with her.

I know this can be a difficult one, but ask yourself: *'Do I want to be right or do I want to be happy?'*

When you are communicating with your partner and she begins criticising you or judging you, ask yourself if it's possible she is coming across this way because she is feeling unloved. Look at the human behind the behaviour and try to assess what might be happening for her.

Is she feeling misunderstood? Is she feeling unimportant or uncared for? Is she feeling unsure of herself, lacking in confidence about what she's doing, or insecure? Is she trying to connect with you and resolve differences to maintain a healthy relationship?

Then ask yourself: *Will what I say or do next come across as loving or unloving?*

Loving her and communicating doesn't mean you're soft. You can subscribe to these gender stereotypes if you prefer, but you are likely to get the same results that made you pick up this book in the first place.

It's simply not going to improve your relationship. The reality is women are wired the way they are, just like men are wired the way they are.

Both parties have to cater to the other person's emotional wants and needs to get their own emotional wants and needs met.

You must be her friend as well as her partner. What would her best friend do? Listen. Support. Understand.

Chapter Ten

When two worlds ALIGN

CREATING A RELATIONSHIP THAT LIFTS YOU BOTH, RATHER THAN DRAGS YOU DOWN.

The needs of both sexes are the same. How those needs are met are complete polar opposites, which is why relationships tend to get so complicated.

To get out of the cycle of 'I'll hurt you because you hurt me' someone has to step up and make the change. The definition of madness is doing the same thing over and over again and expecting a different result. We all know that. However, it can be difficult to swallow your pride and make the first step.

If this is the case and you don't want to be that person because you just don't think it should be you or you are stuck in a rut of believing your partner should be the one to change, then ask yourself this:

What do I want? Is what we're doing as a couple moving us closer to where we want to be or further away?

Just as my friend did with her ex-husband, she had to look beyond what he hadn't been doing for her. She had to let go of the hurt and resentment from the relationship ending and focus on what he *was* doing for her in the present moment, and acknowledge that. She had to look beyond the old reference points of him she had and look for reasons to respect him right now.

If you are a woman, try to do this for your man and see what happens in return.

And if you are a man, you will also need to look beyond what your partner is doing and show her reasons why you love her. She will need proof of your love and you will need to find many different ways of showing her. If she is stuck in complaining and criticising you, there will be a time period where you will need to look beyond that by trying to understand and hear what she's saying, learn to apologise for your part in the problem and ask her how you can help to change the situation.

This will mean so much to her.

It might be difficult in a lot of cases to look beyond the habitual behaviours that have irritated you for so long, but I promise you in most cases, you will be surprised with the results once you do.

In addition to the ways in which a man and woman think and how to address these ways, there is also another fabulous book I've come across by author Gary Chapman, called: *The 5 Love Languages*.

Gary introduces us to five ways we all want to be shown love. He writes that each of us have a primary language we prefer to be used to show this love. Quoted from his website at www.5LoveLanguages.com, they are:

- Quality time – This language is all about giving the other person your undivided attention.
- Words of affirmation – This language uses words to affirm other people.
- Gifts – For these people what makes them feel most loved is to receive a gift.
- Acts of Service – For these people actions speak louder than words.
- Physical touch – To this person, nothing speaks more deeply than appropriate touch.

If you've not read this book, I highly recommend it for further insight into how your partner ticks. Once you've figured out which one of these is your partner's love language, you can then incorporate what you've learnt in this book to help show your partner the love or respect they are after.

For example, for men:
- You might spend more time with your partner by turning the TV off and talking to her or telling her that you want to spend time with just you and her.
- You might give her reassurance by verbally telling her often how much you love her and why. The why part will likely mean the most to her.
- You might buy her little gifts that make her feel special.
- You might do more for her around the house or hand her a glass of wine, show her the couch and tell her you're going to make dinner tonight.
- You might give her a massage, hug her more often, or give her a loving touch as you walk past her in the kitchen or in the hallway.

For women:
- You might ask your partner if he would like you to come out and keep him company while he tinkers with his bike, car or while he builds something.
- You might tell him often how much you appreciate what he does for you and the family.
- You might give him gifts that show him you respect his work or his hobbies.
- You might make his lunch for work or if you already do, you might make him something special to show him that you appreciate him working. You might tell him to put his feet up while you do everything for the evening (even though you are really worn out yourself).

- Believe it or not, some men love to be affectionate and your physical touches might mean the world to him. Why not try a massage, or more sex to show him that you love him?

For more information on how the five love languages work, I highly recommend you go onto Chapman's site and take a look, or buy his book.

REMEMBER WHY YOU ARE IN YOUR RELATIONSHIP

I'd like to share a story with you that has been circulating the internet for many years. You may have heard multiple versions, but the origin of this story still remains a mystery:

> *When I got home that night as my wife served dinner, I held her hand and said, "I've got something to tell you." She sat down and ate quietly. Again I observed the hurt in her eyes.*
>
> *Suddenly I didn't know how to open my mouth. But I had to let her know what I was thinking. I want a divorce. I raised the topic calmly.*
>
> *She didn't seem to be annoyed by my words, instead she asked me softly, why?*
>
> *I avoided her question. This made her angry. She threw away the chopsticks and shouted at me. "You're not a man!" That night, we didn't talk to each other. She was weeping. I knew she wanted to find out what had happened to our marriage. But I could hardly give her a satisfactory answer; she had lost my heart to Jane. I didn't love her anymore. I just pitied her.*
>
> *With a deep sense of guilt, I drafted a divorce agreement which stated she could own our house, our car and a 30 percent stake at my company.*
>
> *She glanced at it and then tore it into pieces. The woman who had spent twenty years of her life with me had become a stranger. I felt*

sorry for her wasted time, resources and energy but I could not take back what I had said for I loved Jane so dearly.

Finally she cried loudly in front of me which was what I had expected to see. To me her cry was actually a kind of release. The idea of divorce which had obsessed me for several months seemed to be firmer and clearer now.

The next day, I came back home very late and found her writing something at the table. I didn't have supper but went straight to sleep and fell asleep very fast because I was tired after an eventful day with Jane.

When I woke up, she was still there at the table writing. I just did not care so I turned over and was asleep again.

In the morning she presented her divorce conditions. She didn't want anything from me, but needed a month's notice before the divorce. She requested that in that one month we both struggle to live as normal a life as possible. Her reasons were simple; our son had his exams in a month's time and she didn't want to disrupt him with our broken marriage.

This was agreeable to me. But she had something more. She asked me to recall how I had carried her into our bridal room on our wedding day.

She requested that every day for the month's duration I carry her out of our bedroom to the front door every morning. I thought she was going crazy. Just to make our last days together bearable I accepted her odd request.

I told Jane about my wife's divorce conditions. She laughed loudly and thought it was absurd. "No matter what tricks she applies, she has to face the divorce" she said scornfully.

My wife and I hadn't had any body contact since my divorce intentions were explicitly expressed. So when I carried her out on the first day, we both appeared clumsy.

Our son clapped behind us. "Daddy is holding mummy in his arms". His words brought me a sense of pain. From the bedroom to the sitting room, then to the door, I walked over ten meters with her in my arms. She closed her eyes and said softly; "Don't tell our son about the divorce". I nodded, feeling somewhat upset. I put her down outside the door. She went to wait for the bus to work. I drove alone to the office.

On the second day, both of us acted much more easily. She leaned on my chest. I could smell the fragrance of her blouse. I realised that I hadn't looked at this woman carefully for a long time. I realised she was not young any more. There were fine wrinkles on her face and her hair was greying! Our marriage had taken its toll on her. For a minute I wondered what I had done to her.

On the fourth day, when I lifted her up I felt a sense of intimacy returning. This was the woman who had given twenty years of her life to me.

On the fifth and sixth day, I realised that our sense of intimacy was growing again. I didn't tell Jane about this. It became easier to carry her as the month slipped by. Perhaps the everyday workout made me stronger.

She was choosing what to wear one morning. She tried on quite a few dresses but could not find a suitable one. Then she sighed, "All my dresses have grown bigger." I suddenly realised that she had grown so thin, that was the reason why I could carry her more easily.

Suddenly it hit me... she had buried so much pain and bitterness in her heart. Subconsciously I reached out and touched her head.

Our son came in at that moment and said, "Dad, it's time to carry mum out." To him seeing his father carrying his mother out had become an essential part of his life. My wife gestured to our son to come closer and hugged him tightly. I turned my face away because I was afraid I might change my mind at this last minute. I then held her in my arms, walking from the bedroom, through the sitting room, to the hallway. Her hand surrounded my neck, softly and naturally. I held her body tightly; it was just like our wedding day.

But her much lighter weight made me sad. On the last day, when I held her in my arms I could hardly move a step. Our son had gone to school. I held her tightly and said, "I hadn't noticed that our life lacked intimacy."

I drove to the office…. I jumped out of the car swiftly without locking the door. I was afraid that any delay would make me change my mind… I walked upstairs. Jane opened the door and I said to her, "Sorry Jane. I do not want the divorce anymore."

She looked at me astonished, and then touched my forehead. "Do you have a fever?" She said. I moved her hand off my head. "Sorry, Jane" I said. "I won't divorce. My married life was boring, probably because she and I didn't value the details of our lives, not because we didn't love each other anymore. Now I realise that since I carried her into my home on our wedding day I am supposed to hold her until death do us part."

Jane seemed to suddenly wake up. She gave me a loud slap and then slammed the door and burst into tears. I walked downstairs and drove away.

At the floral shop on the way I ordered a bouquet of flowers for my wife. The salesgirl asked me what to write on the card. I smiled and wrote, "I'll carry you out every morning until death do us part."

That evening I arrived home, flowers in my hands, a smile on my face. I ran upstairs only to find my wife in bed – dead. My wife had been fighting cancer for months and I was so busy with Jane to even notice. She knew that she would die soon and she wanted to save me from a negative reaction from our son, in case we pushed through with the divorce – at least in the eyes of our son – I was a loving husband.

The small details of your lives are what really matter in a relationship. It is not the mansion, the car, property, the money in the bank. These create an environment conducive for happiness but cannot give happiness in themselves. So find time to be your spouse's friend and do those little things for each other that build intimacy. Do you have a real happy marriage?

While it seems that this story was fiction. It is metaphoric for what happens in relationships.

"I hadn't noticed that <u>our life lacked intimacy</u>."

My <u>married life was boring</u>, probably <u>because she and I didn't value the details of our lives</u>, not because we didn't love each other anymore.

This is such a powerful message to you about relationships.

Have you forgotten to *value the details* of your love for each other? For your lives? When was the last time you really looked at your partner and acknowledged them for who they are and showed them (not just told them without meaning) that you loved them?

Have you forgotten why you entered into the relationship in the first place?

I'm not talking about the characteristics you liked in your partner. I'm talking about your motives for having a relationship.

Isn't it because you wanted to receive love from that person and to be able to return that same pleasure? Didn't you want to be with someone who you felt connected to, who understood you and who you could share your life with?

When you think about why you enter into a relationship and then compare it to why you are currently in your relationship, is the intention still the same? Or have you forgotten this intention and instead gotten caught up in arguing, defending, asserting, judging, disrespecting, criticising, hurting, making wrong and degrading your partner or allowing your partner to treat you that way?

Perhaps it's time for you to look at the bigger picture too. It wasn't always the way it is now. You didn't always have these problems. Think back to when your relationship first began. What was happening back then?

My guess is that at the beginning of your relationship, if you are female you were giving your man a lot of respect, were appreciative of his loving gestures and you admired him for the person he was.

If you are a male, I suspect you were going out of your way to do loving things for her, were quite affectionate, made her feel special and loved her to bits, and she knew it.

So when and why did it change?

I recently asked one of my clients how he used to show his love to his wife? He said he would often write her letters expressing his love for her. He said she still has boxes of them that she has kept. I asked him why that stopped. He said, *"What, you mean after the move, the four kids, the two miscarriages and my busy life?"*

Time is never about time, it's about priorities! Sure you may not have the time to do all of the elaborate things you used to do or you may not have the finances to buy flowers like you used to or go on romantic holidays but you still need to show your love.

Sometimes I think we have just forgotten the real intention for being in the relationship in the first place – to love and be loved. It's mandatory for a *loving* relationship!

I hear a lot of couples complaining about the problems in their relationships and, granted that's what I'm in the session to hear. However, when I ask them what evidence they are giving their partner to show them that they love them, or what evidence they are receiving of their partner's love, I often get a blank look. Or I will get a slightly defensive answer of all the things they do for their partner, almost like it should be obvious.

But often it's not obvious to your partner why you love them.

How you show your love may not even be what your partner needs anymore. You may be giving love from an old reference point. People change and how we want to be shown love can change too.

A mother who used to value quality time with her partner as evidence that he loved her may now value acts of service more amongst her demanding schedule of balancing parenthood with work.

A father who used to value being the expert on matters around the home may now feel like you are telling him what to do, or are patronising him because you come across as knowing better. He may now value your appreciation for what he does do around the house and how he does it.

We must have a conversation with our partners about how they would like to be loved so we can give that to each other. For starters, try asking these questions:

a) How do you know that I love you? What do you think I do to show you this?

b) How would you like me to show you that I love you? What do you need from me to show you that I do?

See where that discussion leads you. The answers may surprise you because often we *forget to value the details of our lives*. We forget to follow the fundamental rule of a relationship – to love!

BEHIND CONFLICT IS HURT – UNDERSTAND THE HUMAN BEHIND THE BEHAVIOUR

Every single human being on this planet wants to be loved, approved of, accepted, appreciated or feel they are good enough.

We all need these things for emotional survival and this becomes even more of a need when it comes to those we love. We love them because we value them, we like them, we trust them and we have a high opinion of them. Of course we are going to feel like their opinion of us matters too.

For whatever reason, be it kids coming onto the scene, more financial pressure, busy lives, demanding careers, subscribing to (or resisting) society's gender roles, or personal unhappiness, when relationships start to enter troubled waters, it is because one or the other (but probably both) party have forgotten either the art of giving or receiving love and have become selfish.

This has usually come about by perceiving they were mistreated, unloved or rejected in the first place and now their behaviour has become a point of either protecting themselves from further pain (by being defensive) or an attempt to bring the other person down in order to feel better about themselves.

Whenever there is dysfunction in a relationship there is always an underlying hurt. This can be a result of one partner doing the hurting or a past issue that is making the partner feel hurt.

The first part to correcting any relationship that has gone off the rails is to establish an understanding of the hurt. Don't ridicule it, defend it or be dismissive about it. Appreciate it and respect this is the way the other person is feeling and that you can help to turn it around.

For women the bottom line will be that she feels unheard, unimportant, insignificant or unloved. This could be literally from her partner's response to her, because she has an issue from her childhood or past relationship, or because she has taken on too much and is looking for someone to blame.

For a man it might be that over time he has come to feel he is no longer needed by his partner or he doesn't feel like he is good enough or doing things well enough. Perhaps he's feeling discontent with other areas of his life and is taking his frustrations out on his partner.

Try to use the information you have learnt in sections A and B of this book to understand your partner before you begin trying to repair the conflict within your relationship. Try to understand the human behind the behaviour. Try to recognise that, just like you, your partner is looking for love, understanding, acceptance, approval, appreciation and to feel they are good enough.

You can't fight love with hate and expect a friendly outcome, but you can fight hate with love and experience a shift in your relationships.

Rather than bringing your partner down further, try to understand their behaviour and lift them up. Recognise that when they are acting undesirably it is not about you. It is about how they are feeling about themselves and the events taking place in their lives.

Sometimes when I am ranting and raving about my day or the housework Steve will look at me and say: *"Come here. I think you need a cuddle."* He will draw me close to him and even though I may keep complaining while he's doing it, somehow he just gets me to soften and I'm not so annoyed anymore.

He doesn't personalise my behaviour and I really admire that about him. It teaches me to do the same when he behaves that way.

When you realise that people just want what you want – to be loved – and you give it to them regardless of their behaviour you will start to see a shift in their behaviour towards you.

You will find that their behaviour will either lessen in intensity and the space will be created for communication, negotiation and change to take place, or the behaviour will stop altogether.

That's because the person is no longer defending themselves or having to justify themselves. They feel loved and guess what they want to do with that love? They want to share it and give it back.

But you must be genuine with your words and actions. False love with an agenda can be felt a mile away.

Find things you are genuinely grateful for. Look at your partner and reconnect with why you love them and feel it before you say it. Acknowledge, praise and let your admiration be known for things you genuinely like about them.

Connect with the reason you chose this person in the first place. I don't mean the characteristics you were attracted too. I mean the intention of having a relationship full stop.

Reconnect with the intention of sharing, giving and receiving love.

This is the point we want to get back to. Love is what enriches our lives, gives it depth and makes us feel inspired, motivated and happy. If you don't feel this way about your relationships and you are living in a repetitive loop of *'I'll hurt you because you hurt me'*, start using some of the methods taught in this book and learn how to change all that through understanding, acceptance and applying new ways of communicating with your partner.

You have chosen this book for a reason – to educate yourself on how to do things differently. I assume it was to attempt to learn ways to bring back that love you once experienced or always yearned for.

And even though you may not see it, or they may not show it, it WILL be what your partner wants too. It's what we all want.

Sometimes we just need to learn how to get underneath the layers of hurt and protection creating the conflict and reveal that vulnerability underneath.

For men and women this is a completely different approach.

Section C

Creating Change in Your Relationship

Chapter Eleven

**INTIMACY —
THE REAL AGENDA BEHIND ANY RELATIONSHIP**

Marital relationships are supposed to be about intimacy, connection and love.

Look closer at the word INTIMACY for a moment. Listen to it. How does it really sound?

IN-TO-ME-SEE

We are in a relationship to connect with another person on an intimate level – on a level that no one else gets to us on - physically, emotionally and spiritually. We want to be vulnerable enough for a person to see beyond the surface layer of what other people see – to be able to see into who we really are.

I want you to take a moment to recall the words to the great Whitney Houston's song *"Run to You"*

> *I know that when you look at me*
> *There's so much that you just don't see*
> *But if you would only take the time*
> *I know in my heart you'll find*
> *A girl is scared sometimes who isn't always strong*
> *Can't you see the hurt in me? I feel so all alone.*

Sometimes in a relationship we forget to look beyond the surface layer of our partner and we get caught up in the behaviour they're displaying and what we think their behaviour means about our own lives. We don't look at the fear and hurt that's going on behind our partner's behaviour and help them with that. Instead we react to it, add more hurt, which creates more of your partner's bad behaviour.

We stop giving them what they want and need because we aren't getting what we want and need, not realising this is only causing further separation from intimacy and connection.

In this first verse Whitney sings about something that is going on for all of us. We all have hurts and fears to contend with. We have all experienced situations that have caused us to feel hurt, betrayed or upset. We all have fears that deep down we are not good enough for the world around us. We have all been brought up in a world that teaches us that our worth is conditional and that we need to prove our worth to those around us.

In this song Whitney pleads to her man to look behind her behaviour and see the *'girl who is scared sometimes and isn't always strong.'* To be able to see the hurt in her and how alone she sometimes feels. This need applies to men and women too.

This is what I will be encouraging you to do for your partner as you move into this section of the book. I urge you to see that behind your partner's unkind or disengaged behaviour is someone who isn't always strong. It is someone who is likely to be hurting in some way. Their hurt is the reason they are hurting you. Do you want to keep adding to that hurt and thus keep getting hurt in the process, or do you want to be the one who changes the dynamics of your relationship?

You need to begin looking beyond the behaviour and IN-TO-ME-SEE the human behind the behaviour who is just like you.

Just because men are big and strong or portray themselves to be that way, doesn't mean they are exempt from pain or exempt from feeling like they are not good enough. In fact I think I have been able to show you in many cases the opposite is actually happening for our men.

Similarly if you are seeing your woman who is playing the role of wanting to control everything and putting enormous pressure on herself to be it all and do it all and who seems to be showing you she doesn't need you, I urge you to look beyond her behaviour too, as reflected in the next verse of Whitney's song:

> *Each day…*
> *Each day I play the role*
> *Of someone…always in control*
> *But at night….I come home and turn the key.*
> *There's nobody there. No one cares for me.*
> *What's the sense of trying hard to find your dreams?*
> *Without someone to share it with. Tell me what does it mean?*

Whitney so eloquently describes the sense of loneliness that comes from that 'I-don't-need-anyone' identity which is really coming from a place of fear and protection. Fear that I'm not good enough and protection from anyone ever finding that out.

Even when in a relationship we can find ourselves ending our days feeling *'There's nobody there. No one cares for me.'* It's even more hurtful to realise you *are* in a relationship and still feel this way. That the person who is supposed to be there for you is adding more hurt to you and when I realise this, what do I do? I hurt you back. I bring you down so I can somehow feel a little better about myself.

Someone in the relationship needs to start looking beyond their partner's behaviour and IN-TO-ME-SEE the truth that underneath all the façade is a person who wants to be loved and nurtured. Underneath control is always a fear – fear I am inadequate and won't be loved.

In a relationship, the whole point is to be able to share your life with that other person, otherwise what is the point of it all? Love is what life is all about. It's not about hurting and pulling each other down. But somewhere along the lines this intention has been lost amongst that crazy cycle of continuing to hurt one another.

> *I want to run to you*
> *Won't you hold me in your arms and keep me safe from harm*
> *I want to run to you.*
> *But if I come to you…. Tell me will you stay or will you run away?*

Hurtfulness in a relationship comes from perceiving that someone has hurt us. It can also come from a fear of vulnerability - I don't want to show you how I really feel because you could hurt me again. I want to run to you and I want to be intimate, but I'm afraid I will be hurt again.

It's much easier to stick with what we know than to face a fear of something we may not be able to handle.

So we stay stuck in our loveless patterns of asserting we are strong and don't need the affections from our partners and get further from what we truly desire from our relationships, at the same time moving further away from happiness too.

What all of us really want is a safe place to fall when we get home from a hard day. We want someone who will encourage us, lift us up, and make us feel special when we are feeling like we are not good enough.

We want someone who will help us make sense of the world and who we feel safe to discuss our inner most feelings and fears.

You may not express yourself in the same way that Whitney Houston does in this song, but the agenda and fear is still there for everyone, even the tough guys and unsentimental ladies reading this. If I come to you and if I'm vulnerable to you will you accept me? Or will you turn away from me and give me further rejection?

It is this fear and personal turmoil that keeps relationships estranged.

As you move into this section of the book I will urge you to take on an entirely different approach to your relationship. This is going to take some real courage and vulnerability.

It is the higher road less travelled.

It is an opportunity to break the cycle causing discontentment and hurt in your relationship.

It will require you to step up and be the person who looks behind your partner's behaviour and loves them anyway, and at the beginning you will likely be doing this without any return, for it will take time to break your partner's defences down.

There will be times you won't feel like treating your partner nicely because of the way he/she is treating you and you'll be tempted to go back to your old ways. However, I urge you to continue to understand the real hurt and beliefs driving their behaviour.

I encourage you to have faith in their fundamental desire to be loved in their manly or womanly way and keep giving them that love. Eventually it will be returned to you.

It makes so much sense to me now after doing so much research and seeing evidence of this truth in my relationship and in my clients' relationships.

I want you to experience this shift too. I want you to experience the intimate relationship you want and ultimately, your partner wants too. However, you will need to BE the Change you wish to see in your relationship first before you get to the ideal you are looking for.

As we move into the much needed practical section of this book you'll be armed with the skills to resolve some of the very real issues, issues which can't be solved with the romantic words of a song.

However, I will continue to remind you of the driving intention of a relationship.

Because regaining love and intimacy between the two of you is really why you picked up this book right? Well this section is going to bring it all together for you and teach you how to apply your understanding of your partner and yourself and the reality of where your relationship is at, into the space where real connections can be made and walls broken down.

Chapter Twelve

PREPARING FOR CHANGE.
SETTING THE FOUNDATIONS FOR ALIGNING YOUR RELATIONSHIP

The key word to take from this title is ALIGNMENT. We need both sexes. Two halves make a whole. Your partner is not the enemy. They are your equal mate in life. We need to remember to align with them as your equal – your friend rather than your foe.

Always remember your intention for the relationship is to love and be loved.

To do this will require you to be considerate, compassionate, understanding and respectful of your partner's beliefs, wants, needs and ideals, as well as your own.

Historical gender roles have brought us into the present with confusion. The social and cultural expectations for both sexes have dramatically changed in the last century and couples need to deliberately find their own equilibrium - there is no right or socially agreed upon way it should be.

This is a great thing because it also means freedom and choices. It can also mean that between couples there is further grounds for conflict.

Now more than ever there is a need for the modern day couple to speak up and learn how to communicate with each other.

We all want alignment with our partners – to stand side by side as partners. That doesn't mean all decisions will be made by both parties or that we have to agree on everything.

The alignment I refer to is where you both respect each other and treat each other with that respect. To learn how to communicate with each other on equal ground. To be able to consider each other's wants and needs and enter into agreements upon which both of you are able to communicate, negotiate and compromise in a way that connects you in the way you're seeking.

Alignment is where both of you feel equally valued in the relationship. When one person is leading, the other person is happy to follow and both parties are happy for those roles to be switched.

There will always need to be one leader but depending on the topic in question, it doesn't always have to be one sex or the other. Alignment is about knowing when to make that switch in accordance with each other's strengths and weaknesses.

Before reaching this stage of alignment within your relationship there are foundations to be laid. There is some more homework, if you will, that you will need to address before even beginning to get into resolving your problems. The first thing to consider is:

WHAT EXACTLY IS THE PROBLEM?

Think about the issue you are having with your partner. If there are multiple issues think about them one topic at a time.

What is the real problem for you or your partner?

This question will end in you or your partner feeling they are missing out on something they feel they need for them to feel worthy or to live up to certain ideals of a quality life.

"I am missing out on help around the house, which would make me feel respected for what I do and make my life more pleasurable."

"I am missing out on you acknowledging what I do for this family, which would let me know you think I am a caring and capable provider for the family."

A friend of mine was telling me that whenever her husband discussed a decision with her he would always ring his mum and dad and also discuss it with them. His mother or father would often tell him the exact thing she would tell him, however it was his mum and dad's input that ultimately made him decide.

Understandably my friend was offended by this and what caused her to be even more offended was her own childhood beliefs. She was brought up as the only daughter with two brothers who were very academically minded. She was always the non-academic one and never felt her opinions were valid in the family.

Her husband's behaviour seemed to further reinforce this hurt and made her even more reactive to his behaviour.

As she was telling me this her husband was in the room. We had already been discussing his background and he had spoken about his own Italian cultural beliefs about his role as a man to be a strong provider and to respect his parents by working hard. He had been brought up with a very strong respect for his parents and often used them as a reference point for how he should live his life.

Understanding both of these beliefs I could easily see the conflict occurring was ultimately coming from a misunderstanding of each other's agendas and belief systems.

You see whenever anyone makes a decision and takes action, as we discussed in Section B, there is always a self-worth belief component activated to cause that behaviour.

The reason he called his parents actually had nothing to do with my friend or whether her husband valued or didn't value her opinion. It came from his own self-worth beliefs about how to live his life in order to be worthy.

He placed great value on winning his parents approval.

Her reaction to him calling his parents came from her self-worth beliefs that she didn't feel like her opinion mattered.

Really the problem wasn't even about his behaviour, but how each of them interpreted his behaviour.

That is the misalignment that needed to be dealt with.

He thanked me for highlighting the important fact that him ringing his parents had nothing to do with my friend - he had been trying to tell her that for years, but without the evidence to show her the set-up of why it was important to him she continued to believe it was evidence to support her theory of not being good enough.

We only see evidence of what we put our attention on. When you are looking at the problems in your relationship, it's important to be able to look at the beliefs behind why you are so reactive to your partner's behaviour. What do you think their behaviour means about you? What childhood insecurities and self-worth beliefs does it trigger in you when he or she behaves that way?

Similarly, why is your partner so reactive to your behaviour (or decisions)? Are there self-worth beliefs, insecurities and fears playing out on their side of things too? That is the real problem to be addressed.

If my friend was able to communicate to her husband that his actions reinforced her insecurities from her childhood, he may have been able to help her to disassociate his decision from her worth by explaining why he always called his parents – because of his belief that their approval was important.

A conflict of self-worth beliefs is ultimately always at play behind a relationship.

Further examples:

Sex – What does it mean to your partner that he or she is not getting the amount of sex they want? Why do you feel like you can't give them what they want? Is it an intimacy thing? Is it an exhaustion thing?

Try to help your partner to understand your standpoint and try to understand why it's important for them to have more sex.

Money – What is the actual issue here and how is it attached to your or your partner's self-worth. What are each set of beliefs about money and where do they come from? What are the beliefs around yours and your partner's insecurities and fears about money? Where do they come from?

Housework – What does it mean to your partner to have the house in order? It's not about the towels left on the floor or the reoccurring pile of laundry. It's about what these things mean about your partner. What does it represent to them on a deeper level? Does it represent disrespect to them? Does it represent an increasing workload and an unhappiness with the current workload? Why doesn't it mean anything to you? Why are you able to dismiss little things like that?

A classic mistake men often make with women is being very literal about their partner's problems. He hears her complaining about the housework and offers her a solution to changing it. *"Why do you create so much work for yourself?" "Don't worry about it. It's only going to get messy again."*

He doesn't realise she has her self-worth attached to it somehow. By dismissing it and trying to offer logical reasoning, he makes her feel dismissed. He might as well said to her *"You don't matter. Stop trying to make yourself feel good."* She can't just drop it because often she has her whole identity tied up in how well she keeps house, even if she does take on a modern day belief that housework should be a joint effort.

Some deeply ingrained gender roles and expectations are hard to shake.

Similarly a classic mistake women make is nagging their partner to come home from work earlier or to stop working as much.

This was happening to my own relationship when my children were little and also in another friend's relationship. I would ring Steve a couple of times a day to ask when he was coming home and I would get irritable when he said he'd be late.

Often a man defines himself on how much he earns and how he is able to provide for his family. When a woman gets annoyed at him or critical that he is not home often enough, she is neglecting to acknowledge what he is doing for the family and how important it is for him to be acknowledged for his effort.

Telling a woman not to care about the housework is like telling a man not to care about working. They both have their self-worth attached to it, so they literally can't stop caring about it.

I realise this is gender stereotypical again and isn't where all men and women have their self-worth, however for the purposes of an example you can see where I'm coming from.

When you are preparing to deal with a relationship issue, before you even begin to try to resolve it you must begin to understand its true nature.

This is where the questionnaires from Part A can be so insightful. It helps you to see that behind your partner's behaviours are their beliefs which drive their wants, needs, emotions, decisions and actions.

Getting to know your partner on this intimate level and being interested in their perspective and thinking on the issues you are having is going to help you enormously to resolve your issues.

Exercise Four

WHAT IS THE REAL PROBLEM?

Write down the answers to the following questions to try and ascertain what the real problem is behind the issues in your relationship. Do this one issue at a time.

1. **What are you actually angry, fearful or insecure about? Be specific about what the problem is.**

   _____

   _____

2. **What do you believe this problem means about you and your life? How does this impact your self-worth or your quality of life? Why is this really important to you?**

   _____

   _____

3. **Where do your beliefs come from?**

   _____

   _____

4. **What is your partner's perspective on the issue? What are their beliefs?**

   _____

   _____

5. Do they have their self-worth wrapped up in this issue? Where do these beliefs come from?

_____

_____

6. Why is it important to your partner, or why isn't it important to them?

_____

_____

The high road I talked about in the opening chapter of this section is about not reacting to your partner's behaviour, but to instead look at the human behind the behaviour. Search for the hurt or the fear – the self-worth component – to why they are behaving that way and how your beliefs and theirs are conflicting.

Often by doing so you can already see a more compassionate way to deal with their behaviour because you can understand why it's so important to them. If you are committed to taking this high road then you become all about lifting your partner up, instead of bringing them down. This deeper understanding of your partner will lead to you become more accommodating and considerate of why this issue is so important to them.

If your partner wants more help, give them more help because you can respect that it is important to them. Ask them what you can do to help more.

If your partner wants more sex, try to give them more sex because you understand why they really want it and why it's important to them.

Sometimes understanding their behaviour won't even mean you have to change a lot at all. In some cases reassuring them and encouraging your partner will be enough to earn you some brownie points and return to you more of what you are after – more love and respect.

The next step to preparing for alignment in your relationship is to be clear about:

WHAT DO I WANT?

An innocent question, but an important one. I can't tell you how many people I've asked this question to and they don't know.

They've spent so much time rolling around in what they're not getting, they've not really considered what the ideal is. Often what they want is some generalised idea with no real clarity.

Before you even consider discussing a relationship problem with your partner make sure you know exactly what you'd like the new alignment to be.

How can your partner come to the party and give you what you need if you aren't telling them exactly how you'd like your needs to be met?

To establish clearly what you want there are a few things you need to consider:

- **Be specific**

    You might want your partner to be more romantic, but what does that actually mean to you? What does it look like? What will your partner need to specifically do to meet that desire? And how often will be satisfying?

    You might want your partner to stop being so critical of you. What will they need to do instead exactly? What do you call critical and what is the opposite you would like to see? Encouragement perhaps? What does that look like? How do you want to be treated?

    You might want your partner to be home more often and stop working or going out as much. However that's not clear enough. How often is often? Does this mean you want your partner home every night? Does this mean it's okay for them to be out Mondays and Fridays, but nothing else?

If you want more time out, how much time do you need? How long and how often?

It's not enough to just consider what you want. You also need to think about how it will look when you get it. Going into bat for something you want with your partner means they will need to know exactly what they're agreeing to. It has to be clear, measurable and do-able for your partner.

Often, and this is especially so with women, requests fall by the wayside because there haven't been any clear guidelines to follow. You may have just been complaining about how much time out you lack and how you need more time to yourself, but you haven't literally said: *"I need more time out so this Friday I'm going out for dinner with some friends (or drinks with the boys). Would that work for you to look after the kids?"*

Or,

"I've decided that I might take up netball to get a bit more time out and do something for myself. I've looked it all up and the commitment is every Wednesday night. Do you think you could arrange to come home early from work that day?"

With women being talkers they often share their problems and like to 'talk it out'. Men are often so used to her complaining and rejecting his attempts to help solve the problem, he has become immune to what he deems is her whingeing and probably doesn't even know the conversation he just had was her asking him to do something different.

A clear request of what you want and how that will look can make a big difference to conflict resolution.

The best way to achieve a goal is to have one in the first place. How will your partner know that they are helping you reach your ideal if you don't even know what that ideal is?

- **Is it realistic or is it fair?**

    Now you have considered what your ideal is of the situation and you are being specific about it, try to look at how this ideal might come to fruition. Consider your partner's role and their current responsibilities. Is what you are asking for fair? Is it do-able?

    Be prepared to answer these questions because if your partner doesn't think it is realistic or fair, you will need evidence to present why you think it is.

    Explain how you see it happening. Show him or her how it could work and why you think it is fair. Don't forget to acknowledge and respect their right to disagree with you though.

    Also, contemplate your current dynamic. How has it been set up that you are even experiencing this issue? How did you contribute to this problem being the way it is? Did you once agree to the role that you are currently playing?

    For example, if you are aiming to align with your partner to get more help around the house, did you inadvertently contribute to the dynamic that it was mainly your job? Do you need to acknowledge this as you go into negotiations?

    Perhaps you used to do all the housework when you were a stay at home parent, but now you are a working one you would like to share that role. You must acknowledge that things have changed and a new alignment needs to be made as your partner may be just habitually playing the same roles you helped set up initially.

    Is your role change fair and in alignment with your current reality?

- **How will your partner feel about this request? Does it go against their integrity, morals and values? Will it grate upon their self-worth issues by doing it?**

    Think about how your partner will respond to your request. Will it be difficult for them to meet your ideal because of what they believe? Ascertaining this perspective will help you to change how you submit your request.

For example you might say: *"I know you find it difficult to come home from work early because you value your job so much, but it would really mean the world to me to be able to take Wednesdays off to do something for myself. Is it possible we can work something out so I can take some other time out? I really need it."*

Or you might say: *"Honey I know it is hard for you to spend time away from the kids, but it would mean so much to me if you came with me to this work event. I really value your support."*

By pre-empting what your partner's perspective might be in response to your request you can identify a potential problem and go into your negotiations ready to acknowledge their perspective and work with it.

Be prepared that your request just may not sit within their belief system and they may not be comfortable giving you what you want. You may need to be willing to negotiate or compromise.

- **Are you flexible about the way you get what you want? Are you prepared to negotiate or compromise?**

Before discussing what you want, consider how set you are on it happening.

Following on from the last point, if your partner is not comfortable with what you are requesting or it goes against their beliefs in some way, what is your back up plan?

Is there another way you can still get what you want while your partner gets what they want?

For example, you may want to go back to work, but your partner's cultural and family beliefs may be that they believe a parent needs to be at home with the children. If your partner is unwilling to compromise is there a way you can? Can you study while at home for a job you can do from home or when the children are at school? Is there a way you can work some time when he is home to look after the children? If working was a way for you to do something for yourself is there something else you could do instead to get your individual space instead of working?

Sometimes a problem involves one partner having to compromise out of respect to the other person's beliefs. That's why it is good to get an understanding of your partner's beliefs about life and how they have been set up from their upbringing. Perhaps what you are campaigning for just doesn't mean as much to you as it does to your partner.

The key question to ask when compromising is, will I be resentful if what I want doesn't happen? Will I be happy to continue on with life with this compromise? Does it grate upon my own integrity, morals, values and self-worth attachments? More on compromise will be discussed in the next chapter.

- **Know what your deal breakers are**

    A deal breaker is something that is non-negotiable for you. There is no compromise. There is no negotiation. If it occurs then you are willing to walk away from the relationship.

    A deal breaker is usually a mandatory request you have for the relationship that if broken it would severely conflict with your morals, integrity or values.

    Be sure to know what yours are so you can communicate that with your partner. Common deal breakers are often things like no cheating, no hitting, religious or cultural rituals or goals, or wanting to maintain your career after becoming a parent.

Sometimes your deal breakers change after having children. For example, it may have been acceptable and even slightly amusing for your partner to get angry and put you down or throw things around, however now you have children and they are witness to that, it may not be so endearing. You may wish to change this into a deal breaker, however you must communicate that with your partner.

Exercise Five

WHAT DO I WANT?

Take an aspect of your relationship you are feeling challenged by. Answer the following questions. If you are able to, perhaps make some time with your partner to ask him/her these questions too.

You might be surprised by how much insight you get into yourself and your partner when you do this. However, if the communication between you and your partner is really poor it might be best to wait until you move through the rest of this book before discussing this with your partner.

1. **What is the ideal of the situation? Be very clear and specific.**

2. **Why does this mean so much to you? How will it add to your life?**

3. **What can your partner do to help you to reach this ideal - be specific?**

4. **Is your request realistic or is it fair?**

5. How will your partner feel about this request? Does it go against their integrity, morals and values? Will it grate upon their self-worth issues by doing it?

_____

_____

6. Are you flexible about the way you get what you want? Are you prepared to negotiate or compromise?

_____

_____

Taking the high road

In regards to wants and needs, taking the higher road in your relationship might mean you need to step out of the world of you and what you want and need, and get interested about what your partner wants.

If they are behaving in a way that is hurtful then they too are hurting in some way. Perhaps their behaviour is coming from a place of unhappiness or discontentment with their own life?

Ask your partner if they are happy and what they would like to change about their lives. Ask them if there is anything you can do to help them reach their ideals, and then do it.

It will mean so much to them that you have offered and will begin the process of softening them.

If there has been some long term resentment this softening may take some time.

Another client I've been working with admitted he had been disengaged from his home environment for quite a while and his wife's resentment towards him was evident. She treated him with a lot of disrespect and disdain.

However, he could recognise this and rose beyond it. He realised a few weeks of taking the high road is not enough of a new reference point for her to realise he had changed and undo the many years of disengagement.

However, he could see his efforts to look beyond her behaviour and instead love and nurture the human was producing some results. He hadn't yet reached his ideal, but he was already receiving the evidence that progress was being made.

As I mentioned at the beginning of this section, it is going to take some time for the high road to produce some long term fruits of your labour but this needs to be done for your relationship to change if there is only one of you reading this book and following the exercises.

Look for the little wins in how the relationship is changing. Notice how your partner responds to your efforts and how this effects their treatment of you.

Another client of mine had a relationship that had become very distant. Every night she would be in one room and he would be in another. They would even check in with where each other would be so they could be sure they were in separate rooms.

I was teaching her how to show him more respect and to recognise her little wins. She was trying it sporadically, but was noticing some tiny differences when she was being more attentive to his needs. One morning, after a particularly rough night getting up and down with her toddler, her partner said: *"Thanks for getting up last night. I really appreciate it."*

While this was a clear shift in his behaviour towards her, she did not see it. In fact she was annoyed with him because she saw it as him implying it was her job to do it and she barely acknowledged his appreciation.

What a difference it would've made if she had of said in return, *"That's okay. I know you have to work too. One of us has to get some sleep. No point in both of us getting up and down. By the way, thank you for your appreciation. That really meant a lot to me"*

He would've felt good about himself that she was thinking of him, respecting his need to work and also feeling appreciated for the gesture of appreciating her. It would've given him more motivation and drive to want to continue saying things like that to her again. As we continued our conversation about ways in which my client could continue showing him more respect and appreciation, she began to fear she would need to become a Stepford wife (based on a novel where the wives in the community of Stepford dote on their husbands and remain subservient to them).

Here is where the fear can come in from both couples. Women fear being subordinate to their partners and men fear losing their authority, which they've been indoctrinated to believe should be the case.

However, I assured her this would not be the case if she continued to apply the methods I was teaching her.

I literally said to her, *"Good. You might need to become a bit of a Stepford wife for a while to break down those barriers. Give it a go and see what happens. I bet you'll find you are getting a much closer relationship and a lot more consideration shown to you by showing him more respect. He'll want to love you more and will make more of an effort. He already is. You already have some evidence of this. Keep going!"*

Taking the high road will mean you will have to do the exact opposite of what you have been doing. Remember you cannot get what you want by depriving your partner of what they want.

We all want love, respect and appreciation. We all need these things to be able to connect and be intimate with one another. You must be the one to bring these things back into the relationship by taking the high road.

Chapter Thirteen

EFFECTIVE COMMUNICATION STRATEGIES

Now we start to set the scene for real changes to be made.

You have come a long way in this book before you've even begun to get to the practical part of communicating with your partner.

Most of the work so far has all been about understanding.

Perhaps you have already been making some changes to your relationship or opening up the communication channels more effectively, but keep becoming stuck in conflict.

It is so easy for men and women to misunderstand each other when they are talking because their love languages are so very different. Our interpretations on life are so very different.

This chapter will give you some general tips for effectively communicating with your partner, but also some more specialised rules for dealing with your male or female partner. While again this lends itself to falling into those gender stereotypes, it is still valuable to offer these insights because many of us will relate to these roles in some way.

SETTING THE STAGE FOR EFFECTIVE COMMUNICATION

Once again, before commencing the conversation for creating alignment in your relationship a strong foundation must be set. Consider the following tips for guiding your conversations in the right direction, especially if you are about to discuss some major areas of conflict in your relationship:

- **Establish some fair rules**
  Before you begin, establish what the rules are for how you communicate with each other.
  - Things you mustn't do - no swearing, yelling or put downs. Let the other one finish talking. If you need to, grab an object you can use as a talking stick. When the person holding the stick is talking the other person's job is to listen.
  - Contemplate what the other person is saying and try to understand their perspective as simply their perspective and not an indication of your worth.

- **Find the right time to hold the conversation**
  When your partner comes home from a hard day at work, the kids are in 'arsenic hour' and everything's crazy, is not the time to be discussing the need for more respect or appreciation, or asking your partner to do more housework.

  Set up a time where you are both relaxed and open to having a conversation such as this. Perhaps this is a time where you can get the kids baby sat and can go out for dinner, or stay at home and relax with a glass of wine. Make sure when you set up that time that both of you are clear this time will be about working on your relationship. That way neither of you are surprised when the conversation gets entered into because you knew it was coming.

- **Create an intention for the conversation before you start**
  What do you intend to achieve with this conversation? Are you just opening the discussion? Are you hoping to re-negotiate some terms of your relationship? Are you just getting a feel for your partner's viewpoints on the topic before you negotiate any changes?

What attitude are you determined to maintain throughout the conversation? Deliberately align yourself with your intention of the conversation and commit to maintaining your intended attitude regardless of what is said. (e.g. I intend to stay calm and rational).

What do we intend to talk about and what outcome are we looking for? When a relationship has multiple issues it might be helpful for you and your partner to have an issues box where you can each write down an issue to be discussed and put it in the box. During your allocated chat times, you can set an intention to solve one or two issues and draw it randomly out of the box.

Setting an intention for the conversation gives you a reference point for staying on target with what you are hoping to achieve. It will help you to see when you are deviating from your desired intention and guide you to get back on track.

- **Gently ease into a conversation to avoid defensiveness**
Before you initiate a conversation, deliberately think of ways to ease into the conversation rather than getting straight to the guts of it and potentially catching your partner by surprise, especially if you haven't specifically planned the time to chat about these issues.

If your partner it thinking, *"Where on earth did this come from"*, their confusion may cloud their ability to give you concise answers or work with you on a solution. They may automatically be defensive and reacting to your initial statement.

Try conversation such as: *"I've been reading this book and it's been talking about how to try and understand how your partner is thinking about things before trying to resolve issues. What do you think are the issues we need to deal with as a couple?"* or *"What is your opinion on this issue we seem to be having lately?"*

OR

"In this book I was reading it was saying that men and women often think like xxx. Is this how you think about these things too?"

- **Know what you want**
  As we spoke about in detail in the last chapter, go into this conversation, not just with a clear intention, but a specific understanding of what you want, why it's important to you, an understanding of the beliefs you have behind it and some forethought into what might be happening from your partner's perspective. Be ready to be flexible and willing to discuss the matter, rather than just expecting to get what you want just because you want it. Remember the high road is about creating alignment, not demanding it.

- **Create a safe space for your partner to talk openly**
  If you have been judgemental or critical of your partner's perspective chances are they may not feel it's safe to vulnerably share with you what's happening for them. Your partner might be guarded about discussing these issues, knowing how these discussions have ended in the past.

  Remember, we are always making decisions and taking action with a 'What's in it for me?' agenda - the pursuit of pleasure and avoidance of pain. Why would your partner want to discuss something with you that would open him or her up to more ridicule and put downs?

  If you have been unapproachable in the past you may need to set the tone of the conversation by inviting your partner to discuss things openly with you. You might say, *"I know in the past when we've tried to discuss things I have been very critical and narrow minded. I have been reading how to change that and I really want to hear what's been happening for you. I promise I'll try not to be self-righteous or judgemental, but if you feel I am being that way I want you to be able to let me know."*

General tips on how to communicate effectively

- **Understanding the other person's behaviour**

  When you can separate yourself from the behaviour of the other person by understanding the priority belief and the self-worth component behind behaving that way in the first place, then you tend to approach the situation differently. This is because you understand the reasoning behind the behaviour and detach from that behaviour meaning anything about you personally.

  If you're not sure what the agenda or priority is then ask your partner in a non-attacking way, from an interest in understanding them, not to judge them. **Use "I" statements to talk about your feelings**

  Rather than saying things like, *"You do this"*, or *"You never......"*, or *"I hate it when you...."*, instead it is better to say *"I feel like......"*, or *"When this happens, this is how I feel about it."*

  When you are discussing an issue you have, keep it about you not about what the other person is doing wrong. You want to try and avoid any language that might make the other person feel they are being attacked.

- **Try not to say '*Why did you do that?*'**

  As soon as you ask someone why they did something you are asking them to defend their actions and often their character too. If you want to know why, ask *"What was happening for you just then"* or *"what were the thoughts going on in your mind when you did that."*

- **Repeat back what the other person has said**

  Statements such as *"So what you're saying is......"*, or *"What I'm hearing you say is......."*

  What this does is acknowledges the other person and lets them know you are listening to what they are saying. When you really hear what someone has to say, it helps them to hear what you have to say because they are not concentrating on getting their point across.

Also, if you have misunderstood what they are saying then it gives them an opportunity to be clearer and to explain it differently.

- **Take responsibility for your part in the problem**
  Both of you are continuously integrating your individual beliefs to create alignment and harmonious interactions with each other. Each of you play a role within the relationship and you have both participated in setting up the problem that is now present. Acknowledge your part in the problem and communicate your willingness to negotiate and find solutions to the problem. In essence, don't just blame the other person.

  Say things like, *"I can really see what you're saying. I didn't realise I made you feel that way. I'm really sorry."* Or *"I can understand how you have come to see me that way. I have been a bit hurtful lately. I'm really sorry."*

- **Try to start with a positive before addressing the problem**
  Before you first address a specific problem you may have with the other person, first try to acknowledge something that has been beneficial to you. Be sure to avoid saying *"You do this and I appreciate it, but....."* Because the 'but' tends to negate anything that you've just said before it. It's likely all the other person will hear is the bit that comes after the 'but'.

  For example, use comments such as:
  - *"I understand you do this because you want to help, and I've always loved that you are very thoughtful in that way. Over the years this has been what I wanted, however since x has happened I now realise …."*

- *"I really appreciate that you did 'x' for me, so thank you. I want to acknowledge your effort to help me. Can I discuss (the problem) with you as well?"*

What this does is make the person feel good about themselves before you address the concern you have. Make sure you are genuine in what you say though, because it is easy to see through you being fake and it will just appear as if you are 'buttering them up'.

This is not the intention at all. You simply want to acknowledge how their behaviour has been appreciated, but now you need something different to occur. Also, you are illustrating that you understand their agenda for behaving in the way they have been.

- **Know that it's okay to disagree**
  You don't have to be right all the time and you don't need the other person to always agree with you on everything. Where no compromise or solution is needed, respect that the other person may just have a different view on the situation than you and let that be okay.

  At the end of the day the only reason both of you believe what you believe is because you have been taught to think this way based on your personal experiences throughout your life. That doesn't make either of your right or wrong, it just makes you different. We are all different. We don't need to spend time arguing about that.

  When you do disagree you could also use a statement such as *"let's just agree to disagree"*.

- **It's okay to take a pause**
  Don't be afraid of silence. It's okay to stop, take a breath, assess what has been discussed, think it through, or just realign with your intention for the conversation. Take a moment to think about any important actions or decisions before answering.

Also, don't be afraid of putting a pause on the conversation altogether. If a lot of communication has occurred it may be beneficial to stop and think it through and recommence discussions at another time. Voice this and set a date to discuss it again.

- **Stay solution focussed**

  This is where setting your intention before you begin the conversation can come in handy to help you stay on topic. When you find you are both deviating from creating solutions and alignment between the two of you, bring yourself back to the question, *"so what do you think we should do about this?"*

- **Use questions to get feedback from the other person**

  "What do you think we should do?" "What do you think is the answer?" "What do you think is the solution to this problem?"

  You want the other person to feel they are participating in the solution, not just have you dictate what you want. That will only make them feel like you are telling them what to do. Get them to make suggestions about the solutions.

- **Make suggestions, but ask for an opinion on them**

  If you are making suggestions, or asking them to do something for you, ask them what they think of that suggestion.

  For example, *"Would it work if I did 'x' and you did 'y'? What do you think?"* Or *"I suggest that we……what are your thoughts on that?"*

- **Cater to their self-worth**

  A lot of time has been spent teaching you to think about what makes your partner tick –both from their beliefs set-up from childhood, but also from their gender beliefs. Let them know you are aware and respectful of what is important to them and be mindful not to be

unnecessarily hurtful by ridiculing or criticising what is important to them. Remember the high road.

These are general tips that work not just in marital relationships but can be used in any sort of conflict resolution. Try them out. You will be surprised by how much easier the conversation flows when you adopt these tips.

Now I'm going to get a little bit more gender specific and stereotype these tips a little.

COMMUNICATION TIPS FOR MEN TALKING TO WOMEN

When communicating with women it is important to remember these key concepts:

- Women talk about their problems to connect with you.
- Talking about problems helps her to feel better about herself.
- The quality of her relationships is what makes her feel worthy.
- She is looking for understanding, support and proof that she is loved, nurtured and cared for.
- **Her primal fear is that she is not lovable or that you don't love her.**

Before speaking ask yourself:
Is what I'm about to say going to come across as being unloving?

With that in mind, here are some other tips on how to effectively communicate with a woman:

- First and foremost speak with empathy and compassion for what she's thinking or feeling. Acknowledge that you either know how she feels or you understand how she must be feeling. She wants evidence that you are listening to her. Repeating back what you've heard will go a long way in showing her this.

- *"You're not listening"* or *"you never listen to me"* actually means *"I don't think you understood what I was just saying"* or *"I don't feel like you care about how I feel."*
    - Be mindful of statements she'll make like 'never', 'always' or words that imply that something occurs all of the time, as opposed to sometimes or often. Women say them to express themselves, knowing that she's not being literal. However, men tend to take these statements literally. She uses it as a way to express and emphasise her feelings. For example, when I say to my husband *"I have nothing to wear"* what I'm really saying is

"there's nothing that I think I'll look good in". Steve often takes it literally and probably thinks it's a stupid statement to make. *"You've got heaps of clothes"* is often his frustrated response.

What I really need him to say is, *"I understand. We need to look at getting you some more clothes, don't we? You'll look good in anything you wear."* Corny, I know and she might mock you for being corny, but if you are genuine, she will be grateful for your understanding.

- Don't try to fix her. She's often just looking to vent and share her problems to feel better and connect with you. If you aren't sure, ask: *"Is there anything I can do to help?"* or *"Do you want me to offer a solution, or are you just venting?"*

- Reassure her that you love her flaws too as women are often quite insecure about their flaws, especially their physical ones. For example, when she says, *"Do I look good in this? Do you find me attractive?"* What she's really asking is do you love me just the way I am because I feel a little insecure right now and I need your reassurance that you love me. This is your cue to be genuine in your corny response. There's a reason women still swoon over romantic movies, because deep down she wishes her partner would be that way to her and mean it!

- The only reason a woman would stop talking to someone is because she doesn't want anything to do with them and no longer cares for that person. When you stop talking to her she deems that to mean you feel that way about her. If you do need your space, just communicate to her that your space is about you, not about her.

- Share your feelings as often as you can because it makes her feel more connected with you and that you love her. She doesn't understand when you close down on her. Ask her for support. This is what she thrives on – supporting others. She will feel very loved if you ask her to support what you want. Just be sure to be clear about how you want her to do that so that she doesn't come across as telling you what to do and thus leave you feeling disrespected or incompetent.

- Talk to her about your life. It doesn't always have to be about how you feel. It can also be about what happened in your day. Talking is how she connects. Ask her about her day too and engage with interest about her activities.

- Be the one to initiate conversations about relationship issues sometimes. Make an effort to set aside time to talk with her. Women need to release their emotions just as much as men need a sexual release. It helps her to make sense of her emotions, plus it makes her feel like you care about the quality of this relationship.

- Share with her how you are feeling and respond to what she's saying in a way that makes her feel understood. Statements such as:

    a) "I feel……"
    b) "This is what happens for me…."
    c) "I'm not judging you. I'm just telling you how I interpret the situation so we are both understanding each other and we can create an alignment."
    d) "I understand what you're saying."
    e) "I get what you're saying."
    f) "I hear you."
    g) "I can see how you would think that."

- If you're not sure how to support her, ask. *"Honey I love you and I want to support you, but I'm really not sure how. Can you tell me what you'd like me to do for you to feel more supported?"* Make sure she's being specific so you literally know what you need to be doing.

- Explain that your need for space or time with the boys is a way that men unwind. It's a chance to 'run with wolves' and get back to your primal roots. Help her to understand it's not about her, but it's just about your needs as a man.

- Help her to understand how it makes you feel when she speaks to you with disrespect. Chances are she has no idea it is offending you because she's caught up in venting her problems. Remember to use 'I' statements and validation, *"I know you probably don't mean to do it so I need to let you know that when you say x, I feel y"*

- If you feel disrespected, don't respond by being cold or unloving to her, or by stonewalling her. Be open to sharing your feelings and thoughts, as she will feel more connected with you when you do. Start that conversation with something like, *"I want us to be closer so I want to spend some time with you discussing this issue. Would that be okay?"* Remember the high road. Give her what she wants to get more of what you want.

- If you are making huge efforts and are still feeling disrespected you might say, *"I feel like I'm trying to show you that I love you more and do things that are more supportive, but I still feel disrespected. Is there something that I could be doing differently to help you feel more supported?"*

- Ask her how you can love her the way she wants to be loved. Repeat back what she just said in your words to reassure her that you understood and so you can be clear about what you have to do. She will be touched at your desire to want to make her happy because she'll feel like you care.

- Say sorry. Women love to hear you say sorry and take ownership of your part in a problem. It makes her feel cared for and understood. It makes her feel like you are making an effort to clear up the problems and reconnect with her.

- Reassure her that she is more than her insecurities. Regardless of how confident, assertive or controlling she is, she will have things she fears make her less worthy and needs you to show her you love her unconditionally.

- Help her with her self-worth issues by:
    a) Acknowledging when you think she looks nice or when she's done something different in an attempt to look nice.
    b) Praise and encourage her job as a mother and/or as a working woman, and how she's doing a great job at managing both if this is the case. Parenting is supposed to be her gender's forte and these days women are very critical of their own parenting abilities. Your reassurance of her skills will go a long way.
    c) Tell her you are proud of the way she handled something or how she parents.
    d) Speak highly of her in front of others.

COMMUNICATION TIPS FOR WOMEN TALKING TO MEN

When communicating with a man appreciation is paramount for a man to feel respected. Learn to acknowledge and appreciate his:

- Work ethic,
- His desire to protect and provide,
- His desire to be the expert or the leader,
- His need for sexuality,
- His need for personal space and to 'run with wolves',
- His need to fix problems and make you happy.

A man's biggest fear is that he is not good enough – that his ability to achieve in any aspect of life is lacking.

Before speaking ask yourself:
Is what I'm about to say going to come across as being disrespectful or unappreciative?

Here are your best tips for effective communication with a man.

- He lacks the capacity to cope with loads of problems at once, so be mindful of when you are complaining about multiple issues and whether he is getting frustrated. His frustration is coming from his perceived inability to help you or make you happy.

- When you are just venting, say so, because he will want to automatically fix you. While you are venting, be sure to validate that it's not his fault. *"I just feel like the house is never clean. I'm not saying it's your fault. I'm just telling you how I feel."*

- Be clear about what you want and how you say it. The biggest confusion for men is trying to determine what women are really saying behind their words. Say what you mean! Men are very literal. Don't exaggerate or catastrophise a situation. If you are feeling overwhelmed right now, then say *"This is overwhelming right now."*

Rather than, "*I'm always overwhelmed. Nothing ever goes right for me.*" He won't know how to fix that and will feel overwhelmed too.

- Men want to help you to fix your problem. Help him to realise that him listening to you *is* helping. He thinks his Mr Fix-it approach is giving you what you need (by being literal and black and white about things) and doesn't know that listening will actually give you more of what you need than the solutions he's offering.

- When asking for help, regardless of whether you think he should be doing it anyway or not, you will get a much more amicable response when you make it sound like it is a favour to you. Men like to be needed but they don't like to be told what to do. "*Could you do me a favour?*" or "*Would you mind doing....*" will likely be received a lot better than "*When you've done that, can you do this next?*"

    This tip can be difficult for some women stuck in the fight of equal opportunities, however I urge you to ask yourself again: "*Do I want to be right, or do I want to be happy?*" Do you want the help or do you want to keep fighting for the help?

- When a man needs his space, don't assume it means anything about you. Don't make him talk about his problems. He will come to you if he needs to talk. By all means ask if he would like to talk about it, but don't be offended if he says no. He may just need some time to figure things out for himself first and come up with a solution.

- Don't assume full stop! Women are big on analysing what men say because we are often so cryptic ourselves. "*You women think too much*" is something you'll often hear men say because men are very literal. Unless he is literally saying he doesn't love you or care about you then his disengagement is most likely to be about something else. If he is disengaging from you it's probably not because he doesn't care for you, but because he doesn't feel like the way he does things is good enough. Let him know it is by acknowledging how he does care for and look after you and he'll likely re-engage with you.

- If he says. *"I'm OK." "I'm fine,"* or *"it's nothing,"* it means, *"I can deal with this on my own."* It doesn't mean he doesn't care about you.

- *"It's no big deal"* doesn't mean that your feelings don't matter. It means *"I can fix this. I can make it work again."*

- Step out of the world of 'his behaviour means something about how he feels about me' and actually ask him what was happening for him to be behaving that way. *"What is going on for you? Are you okay?"*

- Get investigative when he does something seemingly offensive that doesn't make sense to you. Ask *"what were you thinking just then when you did that."*

- There's a lot of pressure on a man to be an achiever, especially when it comes to money. Fearing he may not be good enough is where his self-worth issues lie. You can help him by:

  a) Acknowledging how hard he works.

  b) Encouraging him to be more of a leader and rely on him more for his decisions.

  c) Trusting his ability to be the provider and nurturer you know he can be.

  d) Allowing him to make decisions and not judging or ridiculing him for his mistakes.

  e) Appreciating the 'little things' he does even when they are things you would expect in a relationship.

  f) Asking him for tips and advice.

  g) Praise and appreciate his good decisions.

- Let him know you understand his need for space and to be a primal man if that's what he likes. Don't make him feel guilty for doing something he enjoys. Don't play games with him and expect he will know what you want. Don't deny him the liberty of doing what he wants because you aren't communicating clearly what you want.

- Some men shut down because in the past when they have spoken they have been ridiculed, judged or criticised. Be respectful of his opinions and his efforts to share what is going on for him, including when he's sharing his sexual desires. This is just an opportunity to get a better understanding of him. Get investigative and allow him the space to freely talk when he does and he will likely do more of it.

- Let him be right. Does it really matter in some cases that you have the last say? Again, do you want to be right or do you want to be happy? Men pride themselves on being the expert. When it doesn't really matter, let him be right and don't try and argue with him on things that don't really matter. So what if it takes 15 minutes to get somewhere instead of 10, or that there's better parking somewhere else. Let the little things go and instead, thank him for his efforts.

Exercise Six

COMMUNICATING DIFFERENTLY

Write down some key points from above that will help you to remember some effective communication strategies with your partner.

Next time you have an issue that arises with your partner take some time to ask yourself the following questions or write them in a journal.

1. **Write down what the situation was surrounding you feeling hurt by your partner.**

   _____

   _____

2. **Identify specifically how you feel you aren't being loved or respected. What could they have done differently to show you more love/respect?**

   _____

   _____

3. Think about what was going on for your partner at that time.
   a. How do you think they were perceiving the situation?
   b. What did they have their self-worth attached to?
   c. Was he or she just responding in their typical gender way and did they really mean to hurt you?

   _____

   _____

   _____

4. How did you contribute to the circumstances surrounding the issue?
    a. Were they reacting to your lack of love or respect?

    _____

    _____

5. What did you do after the incident?
    a. Did you retreat and make him or her feel further disconnected?
    b. Did you retaliate and bite back causing further disrespect?
    c. Did you bring up past events in order to bring them down?

    _____

    _____

6. How could you have responded differently? Using the effective communication techniques, what can you learn to do differently for next time?

    _____

    _____

7. What could you now say to your partner to reconcile that event and make them feel more loved or respected?

    _____

    _____

Remember the high road! You may have to swallow your pride and be the hero of your relationship. Fight hate with love and you will start to see results!

Chapter Fourteen

UNDERSTANDING, NEGOTIATION & COMPROMISE

WHAT IS NEGOTIATION?

Negotiation is a word that gets thrown around a lot in the area of relationships. We all know we need to do it, but many of us are clueless about how to practice the skill or we just don't know when to practice it.

It is emphasised in any relationship advice you will find as being just as important as communication.

Negotiation isn't something you just implement in relationships though. It's actually something you are doing all of the time. You just may not realise it.

If you want to buy and sell something on sites like Gumtree or Craigslist, negotiation is involved.

If you are a business owner hiring an employee you negotiate an agreed upon wage. In a business you negotiate with new clientele when you show them what you have is what they might want.

You negotiate with your children about their behaviour – *"If you do this, then 'x' is going to happen."* You negotiate with your friends - *"Where should we go away for the weekend? I don't really want to go there, let's go here because…"*

You even negotiate on a subconscious level as you try to lure people into liking you, trusting you and treating you fairly. And finally, as a part of society you are constantly negotiating how you can get what you want in alignment with fairness and morality.

In fact, you have already acquired the skills of negotiation, but you may not have honed those skills in the area of relationships.

Be really honest with yourself for a moment. Do you always treat your partner the same way you treat strangers or work colleagues? When you are negotiating with others for anything - either at a restaurant where you negotiate a nice meal and good service in exchange for money or working on a team project at work where you need to integrate yours and others' skills, or perhaps even when playing a team sport where you are negotiating with one another to win the game – is the attitude the same as when you are communicating with your partner?

When it comes to communication and negotiation it is too often the case that with our loved ones the mutual rules of respect, fairness and morality seem to go out the window.

We seem to expect our loved ones should just give us what we want. After all – *"If you loved me, you'd do it"*, right?

Wrong. Your partner is still just as much an individual as anyone else you negotiate with on a daily basis and the same rules need to apply as they would if you were dealing with anyone else.

The reality is the underlying agenda of all human beings is to seek pleasure and avoid pain. We all have our belief systems we are operating through and we will always try to defend ourselves if we feel attacked. We will always want to make decisions that are based on our best interests (*in the moment*).

In a relationship your partner's needs have to be taken into consideration just as much as yours do when trying to reach an agreement.

An agreement is the whole intention of negotiation. Agree is the key word here, not demand or expect.

Negotiation is the creation of an amicable merger of two belief systems integrating together to create the space for harmony between two people.

This applies in every area of life between one human and another when they interact, so why wouldn't it also apply between couples as well.

Negotiation is not about one person losing power to the other, but rather being able to successfully understand and navigate back and forth between beliefs to create an alignment that addresses what both partners want and need in their relationship.

It's not about always getting your own way, but about being able to achieve the best possible outcome for your position or standpoint.

The art of negotiation, simply put, is to get what you want and also get what your partner wants.

Negotiation is not something that occurs once. It will happen all the time in your relationship because you are constantly interacting with each other and integrating your individual belief systems.

If you want your ideal relationship to come to fruition you'd better get used to deliberately learning the skills of negotiation, because you're going to need them!

Both of you are experiencing life, learning, growing and changing all of the time. What you negotiated last year, five years ago, or right at the beginning of your relationship may have changed by now because new experiences have given you both more information and new beliefs about life.

Sometimes this in itself is a cause of conflict because one partner or the other (perhaps both) are still operating from old reference points – what we used to do in the past – and it's just not up-to-date anymore.

That's why constant communication is needed.

As we get older we tend to get surer of ourselves and start to question our beliefs and make changes to our lives. You may have decided the way things have been in your relationship isn't the way you want it anymore. All of a sudden you expect it to change, but you've not yet communicated with your partner about your change of thought.

Communication is imperative in a relationship so you are constantly up to date with the way each other sees life and what your current beliefs are about things. If your partner has changed their beliefs, you're going to need to know that and vice versa. It's often difficult to accept that your partner is different to you and therefore won't think and act the way you do. Because they think differently they also feel differently, make different decisions and behave differently. But that's no different to dealing with any other human being.

This seems logical, but it's not always something we consider when we are getting frustrated by our partner's behaviour. However, when you come back to this reality you realise there is no escaping it. Your partner is different from you and you have to make a conscious effort to keep aligning those differences forever, or suffer a difficult, tumultuous and unsatisfying relationship.

NEGOTIATION IS NOT ABOUT POWER PLAY!

Going into bat for what you want is not likely get you what you want, at least not in terms of a harmonious relationship.

That's because it sounds already like you're in it to win it. To be right. To get power over your partner or to come out on top.

Negotiation is about alignment, not about getting your own way. Agreements need to be fair and just according to both parties, that's why it's about getting what you want while they get what they want.

Sometimes it doesn't always mean you'll get everything you want either. Compromise is a big part of being able to successfully negotiate.

What does it mean to compromise?

Often the word compromise can leave a sour taste in your mouth because you have a reference point of compromise meaning win or lose or it meaning you have to surrender your power.

The Merriam-Webster dictionary definition is this: *"Settlement of differences by arbitration or by consent reached by mutual concessions."*

We can see from this definition where we get that impression from then. To concede (concession comes from the word concede) means to *"grant something as a right, accepting something as true, or acknowledging defeat"*.

But rather than thinking of compromise as being defeated or losing power, let's think of it instead as gaining something else – the relationship you desire.

Compromise really comes down to priorities. Is it your priority to be right and stick to your guns? Or is it to create fair and reasonable agreements with your partner so you can experience a closer connection. Because if both of you feel like things are fair and reasonable you will make more of an effort to be closer to each other and give more love and more respect.

When one person feels hard done by they tend to fall back into the old cycle of *'I'll hurt you because you hurt me'*. This is where fair compromise often gets replaced with manipulation, bribery, unreasonable ultimatums and depriving your partner of what they want because you're not getting what you want.

When it comes to relationships it's important to keep stock of the bigger picture - what you really want for your relationship. Again, it's time to take the high road and recognise the necessity of creating alignment with your partner and stop fighting for your rights. Instead find the happy medium and show them respect, morality and fairness just like you would bestow on anyone else.

Ultimately in a relationship both of you want the same thing – love, acknowledgement, appreciation, approval from one another and a happy life together.

The reality is that to achieve this you both have to subscribe to negotiation and compromise in order to produce results you both want.

That said, there are some things that are easier to compromise on than others and you need to be sure that what you're compromising on isn't going to impact on your quality of life in a detrimental way that might ultimately alienate you from your partner anyway. You need to discern what is good compromise and what is bad compromise?

Here is my take on some key differences between the two:

Good compromise:

- Even if you don't like the outcome, you can still see it's fair and reasonable.

- When you feel good about being able to see your partner happy or you have helped them to feel better about their lives.

- When the outcome still matches your ideal for your relationship, especially in how you would like to be treated.

- When it still aligns with your morals and values.

- When you can see you will personally grow from the compromise.

- When you can still see some benefit for yourself.

- When you can live without resentment when honouring your new agreement.

- When it involves changing your habits in a way that improves your relationship.

- When you've compromised for resolution, not to just shut the other person up. When this is the case, the issue is not resolved and will likely just come up later on when your resentment has grown again.

Some examples of good compromise:

- Taking care of the household cleaning because you agree that the outside areas, plus your partner's workload, is their responsibility.

- Agreeing for your partner to take a half hour time out after work three nights a week so they can wind down before coming home and engage more with the night time dinner, bath, bed routine with the kids.

- Agreeing to make more of an effort in the bedroom because you understand it is an important way for your partner to be able to connect with you.

- Not going back to work or pursuing your career until the kids are at school because you agree this will be best for them and your partner earns more than you.

- Not spending money outside of the budget because you are working towards an agreed upon goal.

- Stepping back from disciplining the children your way and trying out a different approach as per your partner's suggestion.

- Agreeing to cut back your work hours to spend more time engaging with the family.

- Agreeing to complain less and make an effort to appreciate your partner more.

Bad compromise

- When you are compromising your values, morals and your integrity.
- When you are compromising your spiritual and ethical beliefs.
- When your compromise triggers one of your deal breakers.
- When you won't be able to let it go and move on.

- When you are compromising in order to compensate for your partner's bad habits which are detrimental to themselves and the family – e.g. addictions or extreme laziness.

- When you're doing it to obey.

- When it constantly leaves you feeling bad and like you've drawn the short straw.

- When it's starting to become a habit that you are always doing the compromising.

- When you are compromising due to emotional blackmail and ultimatums.

- When you are compromising your emotional or physical safety or that of your children.

Some examples of bad compromise:
- Allowing your partner to continually put you down and degrade you because they are having a bad day.

- When you've stopped yourself from doing things that are important to you (like hobbies, interests or social engagements) because your partner won't help you or doesn't like you to do these things.

- When your partner is the one who keeps getting their own way and you are the one who winds up miserable.

- When the decision is impacting on your overall happiness in life.

- When you continually feel bad about yourself after your 'negotiations' have ended.

- When you've agreed to give up your career to be a full time stay at home parent, but it's not really what you want. You just did it to make your partner happy because it's their belief.

- When you keep doing all the work around the house because your partner believes you should be the one to do it and you don't want to upset him or her.

- When you are doing something because you've been told *"do it, or else...."*

- Trying to look a certain way that doesn't fit your style or physique because your partner wants you to look that way.

- Trying to be someone that you are not in order to please your partner or appease their fear of what others will think of him or her.

- Having to be dishonest with others in order to justify your partner's inconsideration, laziness or unwillingness to change.

- When you continually have to give up spending money in an area of your interests to spend money on the areas of your partner's interests.

WHAT TO DO WHEN THERE IS NO COMPROMISE?

Difficult situations often arise in a relationship where there is no middle ground. Situations where there really is a win or lose scenario.

One topic that springs to mind is in the area of how many children to have. It's really black or white. You either have more or you don't.

Other topics are what religion to introduce to your child's belief system, or whether to go public or private with schooling, to home school or not to home school. A partner getting a vasectomy or a woman staying on birth control or getting a hysterectomy can be another bone of contention amongst couples.

The important thing when dealing with these issues is to consider the following:

- What is your standpoint when it comes to this topic? What is your partner's?

- Why is it so important to each of you that you have your way?
- Is it a deal breaker for you or your partner if you don't get your way?
- Will the person who has to lose be able to accept their loss without resenting your relationship for it?
- What are the consequences for going one way or another with this decision? Look at the bigger picture of what it will mean for both of you and the family unit to make either decision.

For example, if you are discussing having another child or not, here's what needs to be considered:

- Why do you or your partner want another child? What do you or they feel it will add to their life?
- Why don't you or your partner want another child? What do they feel it will take from their life if you do?
- Can the partner who wants the child live without having that other child or will they be forever resentful of having to give up this option?
- Is this a deal breaker for your partner to have another child? Or to not have another child?
- If your partner relents and you were to have another child are there going to be any ongoing resentments that keep coming up when the going gets tough either financially or during those early developmental years and beyond?
- Will not having the child leave your partner to feel miserable about life and incomplete? Will this impact on your relationship?

At the end of the day, this example is one where someone has to bend. What it really comes down to is priorities and respecting the other person's beliefs on this topic.

There is no sticking your head in the sand with this topic. You have to seriously consider the consequences as there is also another life involved here – the child's.

If, for example, you decided to have another child even though your partner is reluctant, would they want to hold that over you? Will they be resistant to helping you and leave you to do it all? Will they feel resentful towards their responsibilities towards that child or to you? Is it fair to ask another person to have another child when they don't want to?

On the other side, would it really cause a massive impact to have another child? Will it really make that much of a difference to your current family life in the long run? Will your partner be a lot happier with another child and you can make that sacrifice to fulfil your partner's dreams? Will you be able to let go of your idea of the right family dynamic without resentment? Is there a way you could get around your concerns for having another child – like hire domestic help to deal with the extra workload, or set up a plan to meet certain financial goals before trying for another child?

There is no doubt scenarios like this are difficult to overcome and the discussions about them may go on for some time, but when the final decision is made someone will have to give up what they wanted completely.

This will be a much easier thing to do if that person feels the decision has been made with a lot of consideration to their beliefs and feelings. Often situations like this find their own resolution when it is discussed openly and calmly with genuine consideration to each other's views on the matter.

Situations such as these will really be about weighing up each other's priorities and working out which one is the most fair. It will really come right back to assessing those morals, values and ethics from childhood and why each other has their self-worth attached to their desired outcome.

An understanding from this perspective may help to more easily ascertain which decision to make and why that decision is the way to go.

The difference between compromise & negotiation

In summary, compromise is really about knowing what you are willing to give in the relationship to create alignment. It's not about giving *in*, per se, but *giving of* your desire to always be right and always have things go your way. It's about respecting the other person's personality differences and working with each other in the spirit of fairness and alignment.

Compromise is the knowing of yours and your partner's standpoint on a matter and knowing what you will contribute to help reach an agreement.

Negotiation is the act of working with those standpoints and contributions to create an amicable agreement that both parties can be happy with.

As we move into the next chapter, you will learn how to bring these two understandings of negotiation and compromise into action to deal with some of your relationship issues.

Chapter Fifteen

CREATING A NEW AGREEMENT – A ROAD MAP FOR SUCCESSFUL COMMUNICATION, NEGOTIATION & COMPROMISE

This entire book has been a lead up to getting you to this moment – where changes are made.

This part of the book is where you will now be required to act upon your willingness to create a new direction for your relationship. Hopefully you have already been taking the high road and have seen an increase in your partner's willingness to create a new direction too.

You are now armed with the mindset to break the patterns of your old way of thinking and behaving, and thus communicating, so now is the time to put it all into practice.

Be gentle with yourself though, because change takes time and you may not remember everything straight away especially if you are in the middle of an emotional and difficult phase with your partner.

In this chapter I'm going to show you a five step process to help you remember how to put everything you have learnt together. You'll learn how to recognise where you are on the map for change and how to move towards solution and away from conflict.

For now I want to show you the road map for managing a conversation with the intention of alignment. There are six stages to consider.

1. Preparation

We've spent a lot of time on preparation. The foundation has to be laid before you can build a great interactive communication experience leading towards alignment. Let's summarise what is involved in the preparation stage.

Understanding – getting a clear understanding of your standpoint, your partner's standpoint, where your beliefs come from and how they tend to be attached to your self-worth or your perceived 'right' way to live.

Know what the real problem is – what are you really negotiating for? Why is it so important to you? What does it mean about you and your life?

Know what you want and an idea of what your partner wants - What are you prepared to compromise on? Know your deal breakers and your limits for what you will and won't accept. Be prepared with what will be a good compromise and a bad compromise.

Memorise key communication strategies that resonated with you.

Create an appropriate time to hold the discussion - either agree on a time or choose a moment when both of you are relaxed and ready to engage.

Set an intention for the conversation that aligns with your desired outcome for the conversation itself, the desired attitude and temperament you wish to maintain, and the overall intention for your relationship, which is to maintain or improve the love, connection and intimacy between the two of you.

2. Discuss the 'disagreement' with your partner.

Remember the communication strategies for easing into the conversation? Find a way to discuss the issue at hand that doesn't initiate defensiveness from the onset. For starters, it might be better to address the issue as a disagreement rather than a problem you are having.

A "problem" tends to give off the impression of something going wrong or weighing you both down. To me it has a negative connotation. A problem may imply to your partner that you are blaming them or accusing them of being the problem, which will immediately bring their defences up.

A "disagreement" is just a difference of opinion that needs to be discussed and resolved. Starting the conversation by saying *"We seem to be disagreeing a lot about this issue lately. Can we discuss it further?"* might be helpful, rather than saying, *"We have a problem we need to discuss."*

3. Discuss each other's standpoints on the matter

At this stage all you're doing is stating your position on the matter and listening to your partner's. This is where the high road will definitely need to be implemented.

Try not to take your partner's viewpoint personally. It is just the way they are viewing the situation, *in the moment.* That is all. It doesn't mean anything about you personally. Everyone has their own perspective on things and it is important you value and respect their right to see things as they do. Consider whether there is any truth to what they are saying. Have you been doing what they suggest you are doing?

Is there something else going on that is different to what you initially thought? Get investigative at this point. Ask questions if you need to gain further information. Just be sure that you are not asking accusing questions that promote defensiveness.

Remember the way men and women traditionally talk about things. Women can come across as whinging when they try to express their point of view and connect. Men can come across as literal and black and white.

Women can tend to catastrophise the situation using all-encompassing words like "never" or "always" to help her to express her conviction. Men tend to try and fix situations and present solutions right away.

Taking the high road will require being mindful of these gender tendencies and not getting offended by them and falling into the traps of using them yourself. Be aware of the massive differences in how each of you communicate and adapt your approach accordingly.

If you are the only one reading this book it is likely you are the only one who knows this information about dealing with issues in a different way and taking the high road.

You will need to set the standard of the conversation because your partner may not know any other way, other than what you and they have been doing in the past.

BE the change you wish to see in your relationship and don't succumb to temptations to get back into the cycle of 'I hurt you because you hurt me'.

Encourage your partner to try dealing with issues a different way. Be clear about your intentions and stick with it.

If you are the one who has initiated the conversation it might be a kind gesture to invite your partner to start by sharing their perspective first. If your partner is not also reading this book, let them know the new guidelines of the conversation.

"I feel like we are disagreeing a lot lately on this issue. Would you be open to discussing it? Why don't you tell me first how you see things and I will listen. Then I will tell you my perspective. Then maybe we can come up with a resolution. What do you think? Does that sound fair?"

You have just set a new standard for the conversation. Hearing your partner speak first will not only make them feel involved and heard, it is also an opportunity to show them how you would like them to listen to you.

Stay calm, listen carefully, try to genuinely understand their perspective and their self-worth beliefs, and then repeat back to them what you have heard. Then when it's their turn to listen to you, the precedence has been set.

If your partner isn't following suit you are in a position to say, *"I know in the past we have always talked by back and forth arguing, but this time*

I wanted to really listen to what you were saying and understand your perspective. This is what I heard you say….. Would you be willing to now hear what my perspective is?"

If your partner interrupts you, gently remind them, *"Hang on, let's just hear each other out first and then we can get to the brainstorming stage or think about some solutions. I'd really like you to be able to understand my perspective too. That way we know what's on the table. Would that be okay?"*

Get as much information about your partner's perspective as possible so you have a clear understanding of the beliefs. Verbally acknowledge your understanding of how important things are to your partner before you enter into the next stage – brainstorming solutions.

4. Brainstorming solutions

Now is the time to start presenting solutions to one another.

Here is a simple format for having a discussion:

a) Let your partner go first and have them offer suggestions on a potential solution. Encourage your partner to explain why this suggestion works for them.

b) Consider their proposal carefully and think about your standpoint on the suggestion.

c) Respond to their suggestion by first acknowledging their input, for example, *"I can see what you're saying…"* and then advise whether this works for you or not.

d) If it doesn't work for you explain why and suggest another solution and why this suggestion works for you. Again, acknowledge your partner's input by saying something like, *"It's a good idea, however that won't work for me because…."*

e) Then repeat from the top if necessary. Allow your partner to consider your proposal and advise you of their standpoint on the matter. If it doesn't work for them, encourage them to explain why and to make another proposal.

Don't get offended if your partner doesn't agree with you! It's just a difference in beliefs. Respect their right to think differently and continue working on the right agreement for both of you. Remember negotiation is about getting what you want while they also get what they want. It's not about you just getting your way!

f) If you are happy with that suggestion then the agreement has been made. Make sure you iron out the specific terms of agreement and make sure you are both clear on what each of you needs to do to honour that agreement.

g) If necessary schedule a trial period for testing out this agreement so you can check in with the decision made to see whether it is working for you both or not. Don't be afraid to revisit a decision. New experiences provide new information, which often leads to us wanting to change things. You or your partner won't know things have changed unless you communicate that they have so it's important you keep up-to-date with each other and measure your progress.

Considerations to make when creating and presenting solutions

Fair trade

This is where compromise comes in. What are you willing to trade to get what you want and have your partner get what he or she wants? And vice versa?

Alternatives

Is there another way you can go about things? It doesn't have to go exactly the way you initially wanted it to go. All roads lead to Rome. The high road will get you there in a happier way, so flexibility will need to be considered.

Compensations

If you or your partner has to completely give up something important can there be some other compensations made? Is there something else that can be offered as a consolation to giving up what you or they want?

For example, we'll buy this house instead of that house because it is cheaper and I feel more comfortable with a lower mortgage, but when we borrow our money we'll get a little extra for you to buy some new clothes or a new motorbike.

Focus on personal interests, goals, hobbies and dreams

You want to make it easy for your partner to say yes. Know what your leverage is for negotiating a new agreement. What is it they want that you can offer as a trade, alternative or compensation for getting what you want?

What is it you want that you are willing to suggest as a trade, alternative or compensation for your partner getting what they want?

Be respectful of your partner's wants, needs and deal breakers so you aren't making suggestions that will make them resentful of what they want to pursue for their overall happiness and quality of life.

Consider the consequences of the decision

When you come to an agreement, what will the outcome be down the road? Will this be the end of the discussion or will it lead to further discussions? Is this a temporary solution? What impact will this new agreement have on your life, your partner's life and the family's life? Is it in alignment with your priorities, morals, values and personal integrity?

Before agreeing to the terms of the agreement consideration must be made of what is to come after the decision so you are thinking about the whole picture.

Remember that you want this agreement to be something you are both happy with. Be mindful that it may not be initially what you started out bargaining for. The main thing is that you still received something out of the agreement that you are happy with and that doesn't detract from your values, morals, integrity or leave you feeling resentful and giving rise to further issues.

Further grounds for alignment
Something to consider when repairing a particularly difficult relationship is ascertaining whether there is a common goal between the two of you.

It's important for individuals in a relationship to have their personal goals, interests and dreams, but it is equally important to have a common goal that you are both working towards.

This is what binds you and keeps you moving in the same direction. Although you might be pursuing hobbies that don't interest your partner, having a common goal or interest is what can keep you on common ground.

It helps you to enjoy each other's company and keep talking, working together and feeling simultaneously excited as you move towards achieving it.

My common goal with Steve is to own a farm or a cattle station where we can take in kids at risk and help them change their lives. We have many conversations about how that will play out, what sort of activities we will create, what part Steve will play and what part I will play in helping these kids. We talk about bringing their parents in and how we are going to reward the kids at the end of their stay. We talk about where we would like the property to be situated and what we would like it to look like.

It is a goal we have had for years that keeps us working together on our individual pursuits that are contributing to this goal. It keeps him working in his painting business and it keeps me working on the *Parental Stress Centre*.

As well as this goal, we also have aligned goals on how we want to raise our children, what sort of house we want to buy next, where to holiday next, what 'toys' we want to buy to increase our family fun etc.

CREATING A NEW AGREEMENT

Your goals don't have to be big, they just have to be common. Something you are both working towards together.

As you can see there are a lot of things to consider when going into negotiations with your partner. Being considerate of your partner and learning how to still be assertive about what you want and your boundaries requires skill and practice.

If you've never known any other way than to argue, ridicule, degrade or get angry at your partner to get what you want, or you use manipulation, bribery or ultimatums to get your own way, I encourage you to keep learning and practicing this different way.

Start by taking the high road, by treating your partner with more of what they want instead of depriving them. This in itself will pave the way to more amicable agreements because your partner no longer feels the need to defend themselves.

But, as many of my clients have found, this high road requires patience, persistence and practice. It requires you to think beyond "disagreement" and take an entirely different approach.

Chapter Sixteen

THE MIND TRACK TO HAPPINESS PROCESS

Loads of information has been covered in this book. So much so that you may be wondering how you are going to apply it all, particularly during a heated discussion with your partner.

One of the things that would frustrate me the most when reading a personal development or self-help book, would be when I had finished the book. I would feel so inspired and motivated to change myself or my life, yet a few days or weeks later, would find myself right back in the old habits I wanted to change.

I was left without a plan. I was left wondering, "So what do I do?"

I was determined that at the *Parental Stress Centre* we would never leave our clients feeling this way and have created a five step process that gives you a clear way of applying the information that you've learnt in this book.

It's called The Mind TRACK to Happiness process.

The word TRACK in the title is an acronym for the five steps you will need to remember. Here is what each letter stands for:

T – **Thoughts**
R – **Reality**
A – **Aim**
C – **Choices**
K – **Know your plan and action it.**

Think of your each step as a rung on the ladder. The bottom of the ladder is where your stress resides and the top of the ladder is where you are beginning to feel like you are getting closer to your goals and are ultimately feeling happier.

In the context of the topic of relationships, let's see how each step summarises what you've learnt in this book.

STEP ONE: THOUGHTS

All stress is a conflict between belief and reality. Conflict between couples occurs when we don't accept the reality that there are two individuals with two different belief systems that constantly need aligning.

When you are feeling stressed in regards to your relationship, the first thing you need to do is develop a clear understanding of the situation. An understanding of how you and your partner are viewing the situation.

- The self-worth beliefs - what you and your partner think this situation means about you and where those beliefs came from.
- Yours and your partner's beliefs on the 'right' way to live and where those beliefs have been set up.
- How your partner may be feeling disrespected.
- How your partner may be feeling unloved.

Everything you've learnt in Section A of this book is what is used in the Thoughts part of The Mind TRACK to Happiness process.

The questionnaire you completed will become an integral part of the Thoughts step to give you a deeper understanding of what's happening between you and your partner. It will help you to ascertain if there are any other personal conflicts that may be playing a part in your disagreements.

STEP TWO: REALITY

Once you have reached a point of understanding, the next step on the ladder is to accept the reality of where you are in your relationship.

Whether you have one issue you are dealing with or multiple ones, the reality is many things would have contributed to your current experience.

Regardless of how you got to where you are in your relationship, the reality is you are here! Being in conflict with that only causes you more stress.

Before even beginning to work on making changes to your relationship or improving it you must accept the reality that everything that has unfolded in the past has contributed to what you're experiencing right now.

Understanding and acceptance is the theme of this step.

Section B of this book focussed on helping you to do this.

Chapter Five discusses personal responsibility – being able to recognise how you have contributed to the current set up of your relationship or the dysfunction of it. Not from a point of blaming you, but simply recognising that you played a part in the current issue you are dealing with.

Chapter Six spoke in great detail about being able to let go of the blame game. You got a deeper understanding of what drives human behaviour and how priority beliefs dictate behaviour, sometimes resulting in decisions being made that defy logic, reasoning and morality.

You learnt that forgiveness of past actions and decisions is not about condoning behaviour, it's about understanding why it happened, the deeper core beliefs that are responsible for it happening and how to accept the reality of your past and move on from it.

Chapters Eight, Nine and Ten then showed you how to take the high road and change the way you treat your partner. These chapters showed you how to accept the reality of how men and women traditionally think and challenged you to begin seeing for yourself the results of following those guidelines.

The reality step helps you to come back to the present moment, let go of resentment, blame and the tendency to criticise and to stop seeing your partner through old reference points.

STEP THREE: AIM – WHAT DO I WANT?

The thoughts and reality steps are the foundation for creating changes in your relationship. You can't change what you don't acknowledge and accept. It's difficult to search for solutions when you are stuck in conflict with reality, rolling around in a story about how things shouldn't have happened the way they did or how your partner should have behaved differently.

There's no joy or resolution in that path.

You may not like your reality, but you do need to accept that it is here now. Once you do that you can say to yourself, "*The reality is, this is what I'm experiencing, so what are we going to do about it?*"

That's when you can begin to ask yourself – What do I want?

Chapter Ten – When two worlds align - began to discuss what your real agenda is for the relationship and to help you realise that what you both want is really the same thing: love, approval, appreciation, acknowledgment and acceptance.

In Section C you began to look at what the real aim of a relationship is – Intimacy or In-to-me-see – creating a deeper connection with your partner, which we discussed in Chapter Eleven.

These are the bigger picture perspectives of the question '*what do I want?*'

But on a smaller scale, Chapter Twelve began to help you to prepare for change, by setting up the foundations. It discussed establishing how to figure out what the problem really is, the beliefs behind yours and your partner's standpoint and what your ideal is of the situation – essentially what you want the outcome to be.

As you can see, once you get to this step on the Mind TRACK to Happiness process you are already on the high road because you have become a lot more solution focussed, rather than reactive about the problems you are having.

STEP FOUR: CHOICES – *How* DO I GET WHAT I WANT? WHAT ARE MY OPTIONS, SOLUTIONS OR CHOICES FOR GETTING WHAT I WANT?

In this step you want to teach yourself how you can get the relationship you want. The final chapters of this book teach you exactly that. Chapter Thirteen introduced you to learning the much needed skill of using effective communication strategies both generally and from a gender perspective.

Chapter Fourteen taught you about the difference between negotiation and compromise and Chapter Fifteen gave you a road map for how to practice the art of negotiation and reconciling your differences with your partner.

These steps are the traditional approaches to resolving conflict, but by the time you get to this step you are looking at the whole situation from a much deeper perspective.

Your issue is not just about your partner's behaviour anymore. It's been about you understanding, acknowledging, accepting, respecting and appreciating all aspects of yours and your partner's beliefs system.

If you follow all of these steps effectively and consistently, you will be experiencing a completely different relationship.

STEP FIVE: KNOW YOUR PLAN AND ACTION IT

The fifth and final step on the Mind TRACK to Happiness process is to apply everything you have learnt.

Many people read self-help books, feel very inspired and motivated, then put the book down and DO NOTHING! Then they wonder why nothing changes.

Take action! That's what you need to do in this step. I have given you very clear and specific steps for you to start initiating change in your relationship. Now it's over to you to follow those steps (the plan) and start practicing.

You may begin a little shaky at first. You may make mistakes and cause further conflict, but just be honest with your partner that you are sincerely trying to change and keep trying.

Arm yourself with even more information that you can use in the 'Choices step' by researching more information and learning more about resolving relationship conflict and follow those suggestions too.

Go back and DO the exercises I've given you in the book to create more experiential depth to the information presented. If you're anything like I used to be, I would just read them and not do the work. Thus I never got the results I wanted.

You can't just logically get this. You have to get it at an experiential level in order for you to create new reference points on how to interact amicably and harmoniously with your partner. You need to try these things and experience the results for yourself so you can see that they do work and break old habits.

I remember reading a book by Dr Phil once called, *"Self Matters"*. It was loaded with exercises on contemplating myself and how to change. I remember reading over them first, finishing the book and feeling that usual sense of inspiration and motivation. Only to find that three days later it was gone again.

Instead of going back to my old ways, I went back to the book and actually did those exercises. It made such a difference to the depth of which I took on that information and made me feel completely different about myself.

This book will produce a similar result. You can read it through and not do the exercises and experience minimal change, or you can do the exercises and really get it with more depth.

Neither way is right or wrong. It will just produce a result.

The five steps on the Mind TRACK to Happiness process can be used as your guide. Take note of which step on the process relates to which chapters so you can begin recognising which step you're on and go straight to that chapter to help you move up the ladder.

Be mindful that you won't get to the top of this ladder and reach perfection in your relationship - that would be in conflict with reality.

The reality is you will constantly be moving up and down that ladder as you and your partner both experience life, gain new information, get older and wiser, and change your beliefs, wants and needs.

Sometimes when it comes to one topic you'll be right at the top of the ladder. You'll know what you agree on, what the terms of your relationship are and what each other needs to do to make the other happy.

But in other topics you might be right down the bottom and need to work your way back up to your plan.

This is the reality of a relationship. There will always be ups and downs, but that doesn't mean the relationship is going wrong.

It's just an indication there is a misalignment of belief systems and it's time to realign and negotiate some new terms of agreement to create harmony and connection.

Just keep recognising your wins and be real about where you are at on your ladder. Keep practicing the Mind TRACK to Happiness process and you will continue to see dramatic changes occurring in your relationship.

CONCLUSION

Yesterday Steve came home in a cranky mood. He was snappy and irritable at me and I was trying to figure out what the problem was.

Having spent so much time engrossing myself in writing about and researching the principles for this book I became aware I had automatically fallen into a typical female trait – I was thinking his behaviour meant something about me and the quality of our relationship.

At some subconscious level Steve being irritable and disengaging from me made me feel disconnected from him and to a minor degree, unloved. In a sense I felt a bit rejected.

This is because I personalised his behaviour. I'd never realised before just how easily I fall into this trap and don't trust the strength of our relationship.

As I widened back from this irrational fear there may be a problem with our relationship that I would have to deal with, I began to look at what was happening for him instead.

Once able to step out of the world of me and into the world of Steve I got more information about how his day had been and what was going on for him. I was able to hear that he was tired because he hadn't gotten much sleep the night before, how he had pulled a muscle in his back and how his mindset was not thinking very positively because he wasn't liking the job he was working on.

None of that had anything to do with me or what I might have done wrong!

However, this is often the mistake we make whether you are male or female. We react to something our partner is doing without first understanding what is going on for them. We often cause unnecessary conflict over imagined issues that aren't even there or we see our partner's behaviour as some reflection of our inadequacies.

When relationship issues arise we tend to take them personally or see them as a reflection of a wrong experience we are having. The reality is that life is full of ups and downs and so too is your relationship.

When experiences are unwanted in our lives rather than see them as a hindrance we need to see them as an opportunity to learn and grow. Relationship issues are an opportunity to learn how to align with one another, to love and respect when it's difficult to and to learn how to take the moral and loving high road by helping our partner to solve the issues causing them to hurt you.

It's called unconditional love. It's the love we feel that we 'should' be getting from our partner but that we aren't always giving to them.

When you experience a problem it's like we believe we should have been exempt from ever having experienced this problem. But in relationships you are bound to have issues come up. It's not wrong. It's normal.

What starts to feel wrong is when you are in conflict with this reality and you fight it rather than follow the TRACK process, accept the reality of your differences and become solution focussed about them.

When something big happens like cheating, a partner making a big decision without consulting you or some other incident where you are feeling hugely dejected we can get stuck in the shock that it happened TO ME.

We grow up with fairy tales and, as illogical as we know them to be, at some level we tend to perceive our lives have to go in one straight line for it to be successful.

However, this is the massive conflict with reality I try to teach clients to overcome through *The Parental Stress Centre*.

The topic of relationships is no different. There is no straight line to the happily ever after fairy tale ending. It doesn't exist!

Somewhere in our brains we hold onto an '*it won't happen to me*' belief where we think we are somehow exempt from having relationship issues. When these issues do arrive we start looking for what went wrong. We look to blame and ridicule, and we want to make the other person pay for the pain they caused us.

We have held on so tightly to the fairy tale that when faced with conflict we find it difficult to accept the reality that conflict has arrived. You might even go as far as to blame yourself and start to rate yourself poorly because of the state of your relationship.

"*I can't believe we got to this point*", you might say. "*I wonder if we are wrong for each other.*"

Why do you think these things? Because you've come across difficult times? Because you have experienced conflict?

But everybody experiences difficulties at different points in a relationship. It's inevitable because you are both individuals thinking two different ways.

However you believe your relationship should be perfect, at a different place, with alignment and unconditional love.

Fear of not being loved or fear of not living the fairy tale takes over and you put your defences up. You start depriving your partner of more of what they need in the hope that they'll give you more of what you need. You get onto the '*I'll hurt you because you hurt me*' cycle.

Couples think they have lost their way and consider breaking up, but what they have really lost is a reality based understanding that relationships experience disagreements. They've become stuck in thinking it shouldn't be that way. When the reality is, it is that way!

What if this current situation in your relationship turns out to be the best thing that happened to you because it has brought you to read a book like this where you've finally learnt to understand your partner's behaviours and how to align with each other?

What if this very conflict has taught you how to have a deeper connection with everyone in your life because the principles in this book don't just apply to romantic relationships?

How many times in this relationship or over the course of all of your relationships have the same issues been coming up? Is it possible this is because you've not yet learnt your lesson?

Is it possible it is because you have not yet learnt how to accept the reality that disagreements occur in relationships and instead of wishing they didn't, focus on how to deal with them so they don't cause further conflict and resentment?

What makes disagreement move into conflict is the way the disagreement is handled. We personalise the problem, we compare it against this imaginary "right" relationship we are supposed to be having. We stick our heads in the sand and try to pretend we aren't having any problems, while in the meantime resentment grows. Or we continue to be more hurtful or disengage from our partners in the hope that it will get better by itself.

We get stuck in conflict with reality and neither partners are getting what they want.

It just doesn't make sense to do that.

Remember I said at the beginning that this book is by no means written from the pedestal of perfection. It's the reason I'm writing '*we*' instead of '*you*'. I have learnt so much from researching and writing this book about my own patterns of thinking and my own reactions within my relationship.

The common threads creating problems in today's world seem to be a combination of many factors:

- Financial pressure.

- The stress of having children.
- Career pressures.
- The pressure to have more, be more and do more in order to have a successful life.
- Confusion over gender roles.

If it were just these problems causing relationships to break down then all relationships would be breaking down because all relationships experience one or more of these issues at some point.

The truth is behind these surface layer issues is always a person who is unsure about their worth. They either feel they are lacking in love or respect, or they fear the potential of becoming unworthy.

We may fear we may not be lovable, or loved enough. We may fear we could get life wrong or fear our relationship may be heading down a wrong path.

We have to let go of our fairy tale ideas on the perfect relationship and begin to accept the reality that disagreements will arise within relationships.

We need to adopt a new fairy tale and subscribe to a new story that is aligned with reality. A story that goes something like this:

TAKING THE HIGH ROAD
One couple's pathway to a happier relationship

Once upon a time there was a man and a woman. They loved each other very much. In the beginning they were inseparable. She adored him, admired him and appreciated all the little things he did for her. He loved her like crazy. He would often do cute little things for her to show her without a doubt that he loved her. He loved doing those things for her, as it was obvious how much it meant to her. He could see it in her appreciation and the respect she showed him.

But over the years, as they began a family and difficulties arose, they forgot the details of their love and respect for each other and they began to be consumed by their individual unhappiness.

She became fearful he didn't love her and their relationship was going wrong.

He became fearful he wouldn't be good enough for her or ever be able to make her happy. He feared he was not able to provide enough for her and the family – either emotionally or financially.

From these fears they became desperate to protect themselves from further pain. He started to shy away from her and she began to desperately move closer to him by trying to get him to talk more, pleading with him to spend more time with her, to love her more and show her more support for what she was going through.

But this only caused him to become more distant for it gave him further evidence he was not good enough and he wasn't making her happy.

She, in turn, became more resentful and more hurtful because of her fear that her relationship, which she prided herself on, was failing and her fear that she was unlovable seemed to be coming to fruition.

This went on for years, progressively getting worse, until one day a magic wizard appeared before them and showed them another path. He called it *The High Road*.

He revealed to them how to understand what was happening for each other and to see that both of them really wanted the same thing – to love and be loved.

He reminded them that how they started out the relationship was exactly what they needed to get back to – at least in terms of how they interacted with each other.

She needed to treat him with more respect, go back to appreciating him for loving her, protecting her and wanting to make her happy.

He needed to go back to listening to her talk, loving her, proving his love for her and showing her support and reassurance that she was perfect to him just the way she was.

The wizard took them on a journey down this High Road and taught them the reality of having a relationship is to be able to settle the inevitable disagreements that are bound to occur by respecting the other person's beliefs and opinions about life. He taught them to recognise how influential their own beliefs and actions are to the relationship.

He taught them the rules of intimacy and showed them how to communicate with each other, negotiate and compromise so they could become even more deeply connected.

As a result they began to see into each other beyond the surface of their past behaviours and rediscovered a magic that had laid dormant for too long. It had been covered up with conflict, hurtfulness, resentment, bitterness and rejection.

They began to see that taking the High Road was like a ladder that kept them moving upwards, towards a happier life together as the couple they both wanted to be.

Their eyes had been opened. They could both see the error of their ways. They could both see the steps needed to bring them the love, approval, acceptance, connection and appreciation they'd both dreamed of having since the very first time they desired being in a relationship.

Their new understanding of how to have a relationship was clear. It wasn't about never disagreeing with each other. It wasn't about never feeling upset or disappointed with each other's behaviour. It wasn't about never feeling angry or annoyed. And it wasn't about always treating each other perfectly all the time.

They realised the High Road meant accepting one another through thick and thin, working with each other's strengths and weaknesses. It was about recognising both of them were trying to be happy and achieve that in the best way they knew how and to help each other to grow, learn and develop as human beings. They learnt a relationship is about being able to look beyond their partner's undesirable behaviour with compassion and understanding as long as it didn't lead to something that compromised their safety, morals or integrity.

It was about being honest with each other and lifting the other person up when they felt down, rather than stepping on them, and above all it was about giving more love and giving more respect, even when the other person had momentarily forgotten how.

Having experienced this High Road, the couple didn't want to leave. They were revelling in their newfound love for each other. They didn't want to go back to their usual existence. They decided to stay and build their new life on this road, teaching their children the same understanding for them to take into their relationships.

The wizard was extremely happy.

He had taught them to understand the key concept that everyone is always asking the question – 'What's in it for me?' and by giving each other more or what their partner wanted, they learnt it would return them more of what they needed.

He had taught them that the answers to their relationship's success was not about giving up or giving in, but to GIVE MORE!

The wizard had done his job. He was happy. He had created a ripple effect of moving yet another couple onto the High Road.

And with that, the wizard disappeared, leaving the couple to continue their life on the High Road, experiencing a reality based happily ever after.

THE END.

www.parentalstress.com.au

More Resources available from
The Parental Stress Centre

Books

- The Happy Mum Handbook
- The 28 Day Tame you Temper Parenting Challenge
- A Parent's Guide to Finding your lost identity
  (and discovering your personal peace)
- A Parent's Guide to Balance and getting more YOU time

Video Programs

- BE the Change Video Series
  Find your peace and calm, then teach it to your children

- Stress Free Parenting Program
  The rational and realistic approach to parenting that no one's ever shown you

- What's In it for Me Video Program
  The Relationship Repair series

- The 12 week Postnatal Depression Recovery Program
- The Tame your Temper Video Program
- The Time for Everything Video Program

For daily tips and inspirational quotes
www.facebook.com/parentalstresscentre

www.ingramcontent.com/pod-product-compliance
Lightning Source LLC
Chambersburg PA
CBHW070939230426
43666CB00011B/2492